SPURL

DEATH TO THE FASCIST INSE

The Symbionese Liberation Army, a small radical left-wing group based in the Bay Area of California, was active from 1973 to 1975. Founded by African-American escaped convict Donald DeFreeze, the SLA was notable for the following actions: the murder of the Oakland superintendent of schools, Dr. Marcus Foster (November 6, 1973); the kidnapping of newspaper heiress Patricia Hearst (February 4, 1974); the conversion of kidnapping victim Hearst into "Tania," a fellow "comrade" in the SLA (March 31, 1974); the armed robbery of Hibernia Bank in San Francisco (April 15, 1974); the gun battle with law enforcement in Los Angeles that resulted in the deaths of DeFreeze and five other SLA members (May 17, 1974); and the Crocker Bank robbery in Carmichael, California, in which bank customer Myrna Opsahl was shot to death (April 21, 1975). Most of the remaining SLA members, including Patricia Hearst and William and Emily Harris, were captured by the FBI in San Francisco on September 18, 1975.

John Brian King is a writer, photographer, and filmmaker. His works include the nonfiction book *Lustmord: The Writings and Artifacts of Murderers* (1997), the photography books *LAX: Photographs of Los Angeles 1980–84* (2015) and *Nude Reagan* (2016), and the feature film *Redlands* (2014).

SYMBIONESE LIBERATION ARMY

DEATH TO THE FASCIST INSECT

EDITED BY JOHN BRIAN KING

SPURL EDITIONS

Cover photo: The Seven-Headed Cobra – the symbol of the SLA

Published by Spurl Editions

ISBN: 978-1-943679-08-9

Spurl Editions
www.spurleditions.com
spurlcontact@gmail.com

CONTENTS

PREFACE

"The long run aim of the SLA was to work toward the annihilation of U.S. imperialism and the culture and institutions that support it. The building of a people's army wasn't seen as an end, but as a means to achieve popular freedom to build a society that was free of racism, sexism and classism; a society where there were no elites, no oppressive bureaucracy. The SLA wanted to remain relatively small, develop their skills, set up networks in various west coast cities and gradually refine their political perspective as conditions changed. They would test out their theories through guerrilla action, probing the enemy's weak spots, analyze the attitudes of people in their communities as to what would be acceptable actions to take, and check their ultimate response in order to refine tactics, techniques and overall strategy." – SLA member William Harris, "The Last SLA Statement," July 1976

They met in California under circumstances that were typical for Bay Area leftists in the early 1970s: at Fruity Rudy's, a juice stand on Telegraph Avenue in Berkeley, buying and selling drugs; at a Safeway supermarket in Oakland, registering voters for Bobby Seale's mayoral run and passing out leaflets for Cesar Chavez; at a community theater in Berkeley, participating in a production of Ibsen's *Hedda Gabler*; at "Peking House," a commune in north Oakland, hanging out and discussing Chairman Mao and Lenin; and at UC Berkeley, working on an Afro-American Studies term paper that led to field trips to the nearby California Medical Facility at Vacaville to tutor black prisoners.

There was *Angela Atwood,* daughter of a Teamster boss, on the board of the Catholic Youth Organization as a teenager, who worked as a waitress at the Great Electric Underground restaurant in San Francisco's Transamerica Building; *Camilla Hall,* daughter of Christian missionaries, lesbian poet and artist, who worked as a gardener; *Emily Harris* (born Emily Schwartz), graduate with a BA in English from Indiana University, who worked as a typist at UC Berkeley; Emily's husband *William Harris,* Vietnam War veteran, actor in college theater with an MA in urban education, who worked at the Berkeley post office; *Russell Little,* son of a Florida electronics mechanic, who took some electrical engineering classes at the University of Florida before moving into Peking House; *Nancy Ling Perry,* daughter of a furniture store owner in Santa Rosa, wife of an African-American jazz musician and a graduate of UC Berkeley, who worked as a topless blackjack dealer in the North Beach neighborhood of San Francisco; *Joseph Remiro,* son of an Italian mother and Mexican father who was raised in the Sunset District of San Francisco, veteran of the Vietnam War from 1966 to 1968; *Patricia Mizmoon Soltysik* ("Mizmoon" was the nickname given to her by her former lover Camilla Hall that she legally added to her name), her father a pharmacist and her mother a Belgian who escaped the Nazis during World War II, high school treasurer and honors student; and *William Wolfe,* son of an anesthesiologist, prep school graduate and National Merit Scholar finalist, who was finishing his studies at UC Berkeley.

This was the core of the Symbionese Liberation Army (SLA): overwhelmingly white and young, some poor but most from upper-middle-class upbringings. A few of the women were lesbian or bisexual, while the men were decidedly, emphatically heterosexual.

But one of them did not fit the mold, and he ended up being the leader of the SLA: *Donald DeFreeze.* He was the high school drop-out, the fuck-up raised in poverty who got arrested for the first time at the age of sixteen busting open a parking meter in Buffalo – the first of many arrests and convictions that often resulted from his infatuation with bombs and guns.

DeFreeze was the oldest member of the SLA, and he was the only African-American. He had been at Vacaville for a year and a half when he met his future followers on their visits to the prison. With the assistance of the prison's Black Cultural Association and its "outside coordinator" Colston Westbrook (a black linguistics professor with ties to the CIA and their assassination program during the Vietnam War), DeFreeze was transformed from an uneducated minor-league convict into a learned revolutionary "general."

The SLA began in earnest in the summer of 1973, after DeFreeze's escape from Soledad State Prison (a prison escape in which, oddly, no one chased after him). DeFreeze and his two lovers, Patricia Mizmoon Soltysik and Nancy Ling Perry, lived together in Berkeley and created the political structure of the SLA – their name, their politics, their plan of action.

The others later joined the SLA willingly, except for one: *Patricia Hearst,* who was first their victim (kidnapped on February 4, 1974), and later their comrade "Tania" (taking off her blindfold on March 31, 1974).

The life of Patricia Hearst, and specifically her "brainwashing" by the SLA, has been covered exhaustively. What can be noted here, however, is that she shared many traits with the other members of the SLA – she was wealthy, educated, and white; a sophomore at UC Berkeley studying art history, she enjoyed making her conservative parents uncomfortable (she began dating her twenty-three-year-old math teacher, Steven Weed, when she was seventeen), and she even knew how to expertly shoot a gun (her father taught her at the age of twelve so they could hunt ducks together).

The kidnapping of Patricia Hearst was brilliant political theater, reminiscent of Antonin Artaud's "Theater of Cruelty" or, closer to home, of the late 1960s Bay Area "community anarchists" The Diggers. The SLA committed other crimes – the assassination of Dr. Marcus Foster and the Hibernia Bank robbery, for instance – but would they be remembered at all, and have been hunted at the time with such vigor, if they had not kidnapped a rich white daughter of a media baron and made her into one of their own? The cassette tapes and typewriter "communiques" they dropped off at radio stations, underground newspapers, and phone booths were a constant media *drip-drip-drip* that would have been the envy of any 1970s conceptual or performance artist. The theater of the tapes often crossed into the absurd, for the white SLA women usually affected African-American "jive" voices in their recorded political monologues; and to visually record their performances as "guerrilla revolutionaries," wearing wigs and carrying machine guns, the SLA specifically robbed one of the few banks that was newly outfitted with black-and-white-film security cameras.

And the ideology of the SLA? Their most direct influence was Venceremos, a group of left-wing California radicals who organized in 1970 in the Palo Alto area (after the murder of a prison guard during an escape, however, one of the leaders became a state informant and many of the Venceremos members had fled or been jailed by 1973). But the members of the SLA were mainly influenced by what they read, cheap paperbacks that were often found on the cinderblock-and-plank shelves of progressives and college students in the early 1970s: *Blood in My Eye* by the murdered African-American convict George Jackson; *Manual of the Urban Guerrilla* by the Brazilian guerrilla fighter Carlos Marighella; *Revolution in the Revolution?* by the French philosopher Régis Debray; *The Wretched of the Earth* by the post-colonial theorist Frantz Fanon; and the assorted writings of Marx, Lenin, Chairman Mao, and Che Guevara.

Yet the SLA was contemptuous of what they called "armchair revolutionaries"; they thought they were either "cowards afraid of revolutionary violence because it is a direct threat to their personal security and comfort, or they are opportunists who have personal gains in allowing the enemy to enslave or oppress and tranquilize the people" (p. 101).

The Symbionese Liberation Army wanted *praxis,* not academic or political theory. And in their search for praxis, they believed in a leader – Donald DeFreeze, aka "Field Marshal Cinque" – who fetishized violence with very little thought regarding his actions and their consequences. It is clear his followers in the SLA were complicit in their own madness – the media-driven narrative of Cinque as an evil Pied Piper of white innocents is false – yet they thought they needed racial authenticity in their political struggle, and they were willing to avidly listen to an African-American escaped convict because he made their quest for revolution real and valid, even if many of his ideas contributed to their ideological confusion, downfall, and violent deaths.

"The SLA made many mistakes but we must accept mistakes as the price we must pay for our apprenticeship as revolutionaries. These mistakes have to be made now and learned from before the lives of many become dependent on direct and effective action. Those who allowed subjective political prejudices to blind them from seeing the SLA's victories as well as their mistakes have missed a valuable learning experience. Successful revolutionary struggles don't fall from the sky or jump out of books. The value of the lessons learned from the SLA will be felt through the actions of revolutionaries who have their feet planted firmly in reality. People who act like they've never made a mistake are either lying or sitting on their pompous theoretical asses." – SLA member Joseph Remiro, "The Last SLA Statement," July 1976

Editor's note: This book is presented in two parts, each arranged in chronological order: 1) the main works of the SLA, with a supporting timeline of events, and 2) an appendix of letters, newspaper articles, and other responses related to the SLA. All the tapes recorded by the SLA were transcribed by me; I kept the misspellings and other errors of the written communiques and letters intact.

JOHN BRIAN KING

DEATH TO THE FASCIST INSECT

SYMBIONESE LIBERATION ARMY

Angela Atwood – Gelina
Born February 6, 1949, in North Haledon, New Jersey
Died May 17, 1974, in Los Angeles, California

Donald DeFreeze – Cinque
Born November 15, 1943, in Cleveland, Ohio
Died May 17, 1974, in Los Angeles, California

Camilla Hall – Gabi
Born March 24, 1945, in Saint Peter, Minnesota
Died May 17, 1974, in Los Angeles, California

Emily Harris – Yolanda
Born February 11, 1947, in Baltimore, Maryland

William Harris – Teko
Born January 22, 1945, in Fort Sill, Oklahoma

Patricia Hearst – Tania
Born February 20, 1954, in San Francisco, California

Russell Little – Osceola
Born in 1949 in Pensacola, Florida

Nancy Ling Perry – Fahizah
Born September 19, 1947, in San Francisco, California
Died May 17, 1974, in Los Angeles, California

Joseph Remiro – Bo
Born in 1947 in San Francisco, California

Patricia Mizmoon Soltysik – Zoya
Born May 17, 1950, in Goleta, California
Died May 17, 1974, in Los Angeles, California

William Wolfe – Cujo
Born February 17, 1951, in Connecticut
Died May 17, 1974, in Los Angeles, California

CHRONOLOGY

1964

The CIA begins conducting drug research – including, but not limited to, psychosurgery – on "volunteer" prisoners at the California Medical Facility at Vacaville under the name "MKSEARCH, Subproject 3." The CIA program ends in 1972; soon after, Jessica Mitford (author of the funeral industry exposé *The American Way of Life*) writes about the experimental use of harmful drugs on Vacaville prisoners in *The Atlantic.*

1967

Facing criminal charges, Donald DeFreeze becomes a paid informant for the Los Angeles Police Department.

1968

The Black Cultural Association (BCA), an African-American inmate group, is founded in Vacaville prison.

April 1970

Donald DeFreeze receives a sentence of five years to life for armed robbery, assault with a deadly weapon, and possession of a forged check; it is his third felony conviction.

December 3, 1970

Donald DeFreeze begins his prison sentence at Vacaville.

1971

Colston Westbrook – an African-American linguistics professor with ties to the CIA's Phoenix assassination program in Vietnam and an expert on "Black English dialectology" – is appointed the "outside coordinator" of the Black Cultural Association at Vacaville prison.

March 1972

William Wolfe begins volunteering as a tutor at BCA meetings through a program supported by the Afro-American Studies Department at UC Berkeley; future SLA members Russell Little, Joseph Remiro, Patricia Mizmoon Soltysik, and Nancy Ling Perry soon join him and meet Donald DeFreeze at Vacaville.

Summer 1972

Donald DeFreeze is forced out of the BCA due to his history as a police informant. Westbrook gives DeFreeze his own black prison group, Unisight; according to its pamphlet, Unisight's purpose "is to reassimilate and reeducate the black male to the needs and responsibility of the black family and to give the black female an understanding of her past and the relationship between the black male and herself."

December 1972

Colston Westbrook is forced to resign from the BCA and end his association with Vacaville; he later states it was due to rumors about his past involvement with the CIA and the BCA being taken over by "the Maoists."

December 11, 1972

Donald DeFreeze is transferred from Vacaville to Soledad State Prison.

March 5, 1973

Assigned as a trustee to work on a boiler outside the main prison, Donald DeFreeze easily escapes from Soledad State Prison; prison authorities take very little action to find him.

Summer 1973

Nancy Ling Perry moves in with Donald DeFreeze and Patricia Mizmoon Soltysik at their house on Parker Street in Berkeley.

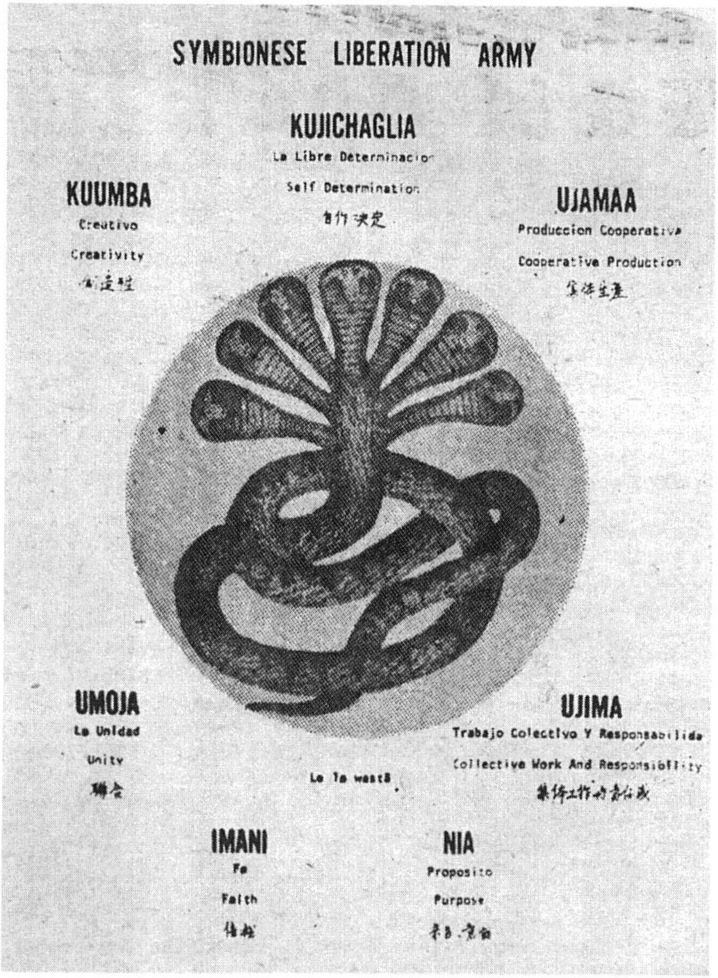
SYMBIONESE LIBERATION ARMY
KUJICHAGLIA
La Libre Determinacion
Self Determination
KUUMBA
Creativo
Creativity
UJAMAA
Produccion Cooperativa
Cooperative Production
UMOJA
La Unidad
Unity
UJIMA
Trabajo Colectivo Y Responsabilidad
Collective Work And Responsibility
IMANI
Fe
Faith
NIA
Proposito
Purpose

THE SEVEN-HEADED COBRA

UNDATED

The emblem of the Symbionese Liberation Army is 170,000 years old, and it is one of the first symbols used by people to signify god and life. The two bottom heads on each side of the Cobra represent the four principles of life: the sun, the moon, the earth, and the water. The three center heads represent god and the universe, and are called the god head. The number seven as embracing all the universal forces of god and life can be traced to the Egyptian temples and their seven pillars, to the seven candles of the pre-Zionist, North African religions, to the Buddhist and Hindu religions, and to the North and South American Indian religions. This is because the seven principles explain the inter-relationships of life, of the family and the state, of the human anatomy and the universe. And because the basic principle behind any kind of union and series of relationships must be equally accessible to all concerned, we see why the seven heads of the cobra have but one body. The thoughts and purpose in each of the seven heads of the cobra penetrates its common body and soul, and from this we see how the source of the cobra's survival lies not in any individual head, but rather in the relationship and unity of all the heads to each other.

The Symbionese Liberation Army has selected the Seven-Headed Cobra as our emblem because we realize that an army is a mass that needs unity in order to become a fighting force, and we know that true unity among people must be based upon a concern that is universal. It is a revolutionary unity of all people against a common oppressor enemy of the people. This unity of seven heads in one body defines the essence of co-operation and socialism in the great undertaking of revolutionary war. Through the puritan capitalist ethics of competition, individualism, fascism, racism, sexism, and imperialism the enemy is attacking us. This enemy functions by means of attacking one race or group among us in an attempt to force us into submission and division and isolation from each other. From these attacks, we have learned that our common enemy will not stop until we come together to stop him, for he lives off the murder and oppression of our divided and therefore defenseless people.

We have chosen the Seven-Headed Cobra as the emblem of the S.L.A. because our forces are from every walk of life, from every religion, and of every race, and by our unity does our strength and our common goal for freedom from the chains of capitalism make true the meaning of our seven principles of unity. Our military and political strength arises from the masses of all our people, for when the people are at one in their inmost body, they shatter even the hardest of iron or of bronze, and when the people understand each other in their inmost heart, their words are sweet and strong.

The seven memberships of our federation are men and women who are black, brown, yellow, red, white, young and old. Each of these members joins together and speaks and fights for the best interests of all within the body, just as one head of the cobra can not be attacked without the others rising to strike with venom in self-defense to destroy the attacker. Each head of the cobra stands in organic need of all the others in order to maintain its survival.

From this example of the necessity of unity in order to survive, the S.L.A. will build and fight for the socialist unity of all oppressed peoples. A cry from any one of us will echo in the body of our common ear, and we will attack out of instinct, and in self-defense, for our survival. And with the venom of our seven heads we will destroy the fascist insect who preys upon the life of the people; and with the minds of our seven heads, and the spirit of our one body and soul, we will secure a future for our children.

THE COBRA OATH

UNDATED

TO THOSE WHO WOULD BEAR THE HOPES
AND FUTURE OF OUR PEOPLE,
LET THE VOICE OF THEIR GUNS
EXPRESS THE WORDS OF FREEDOM

Umoja – La Unidad – Unity – To strive for and maintain unity in our household, our nation and in The Symbionese Federation.

Kujichagulia – La Libre Determinacion – Self Determination – To define ourselves, name ourselves, speak for ourselves and govern ourselves.

Ujima – Trabajo Colectivo y Responsibilidad – Collective Work and Responsibility – To build and maintain our nation and the federation together by making our brothers' and sisters' and the Federation's problems our problems and solving them together.

Ujamaa – Produccion Cooperativa – Cooperative Production – To build and maintain our own economy from our skills, and labor and resources and to insure ourselves and other nations that we all profit equally from our labor.

Nia – Proposito – Purpose – To make as our collective vocation the development and liberation of our nation, and all oppressed people, in order to restore our people and all oppressed people to their traditional greatness and humanity.

Kuumba – Creativo – Creativity – To do all we can, as best we can, in order to free our nation and defend the federation and constantly make it and the earth that we all share more beautiful and beneficial.

Imani – Fe – Faith – To believe in our unity, our leaders, our teachers, our people, and in the righteousness and victory of our struggle and the struggle of all oppressed and exploited people.

THE GOALS OF THE SLA

UNDATED

THE GOALS OF THE SYMBIONESE LIBERATION ARMY

1. To unite all oppressed people into a fighting force and to destroy the system of the capitalist state and all its value systems. To create in its place a system and sovereign nations that are in the total interest of all its races and people, based on the true affirmation of life, love, trust, and honesty, freedom and equality that is truly for all.

2. To assure the rights of all people to self determination and the rights to build their own nation and government, with representatives that have shown through their actions to be in the interest of their people. To give the right to all people to select and elect their own representatives and governments by direct vote.

3. To build a people's federated council, who will be a male and female of each People's Council or Sovereign Nation of The Symbionese Federation of Nations, who shall be the representatives of their nations in the forming of trade packs and unified defense against any external enemy that may attack any of the free nations of the federation and to form other aids to each others' needs.

4. To aid and defend the cultural rights of all the sovereign

nations of The Symbionese Federation, and to aid each nation in the building of educational and other institutions to meet and serve this need of its people.

5. To place the control of all the institutions and industries, of each nation into the hands of its people. To aid sovereign nations of the federation to build nations where work contributes concretely to the full interest and needs of its workers and the communal interest of its communities and its people and the mutual interest of all within the federation of nations.

6. To aid and defend the rights of all oppressed people to build nations which do not institute oppression and exploitation, but rather does institute the environment of freedom and defends that freedom on all levels and for all of the people, and by any means necessary.

7. To give back to all people their human and constitutional rights, liberty, equality and justice and the right to bear arms in the defense of these rights.

8. To create a system where our aged are cared for with respect, love, and kindness and aided and encouraged to become assets in their own ways to their nations and to their communal community. That the life that moves around them is not a frightening and murderous one and where life is not a fear, but rather one of love and feeling and of unity.

9. To create a system and laws that will neither force people into nor force them to stay into personal relationships that they do not wish to be in, and to destroy all chains instituted by legal and social laws of the capitalist state which acts as a reinforcing system to maintain this form of imprisonment.

10. To create institutions that will aid, reinforce and educate

the growth of our comrade women and aid them in making a new true and better role to live in life and in the defining of themselves as a new and free people.

11. To create new forms of life and relationships that bring true meanings of love to people's relationships, and to form communes on the community level and bring the children of the community into being the responsibility of the community, to place our children in the union of real comradeship and in the care and loving interest of the revolutionary community.

12. To destroy the prison system, which the capitalist state has used to imprison the oppressed and exploitated, and thereby destroy the love, unity, and hopes of millions of lives and families. And to create in its place a system of comradeship and that of group unity and education on a communal and revolutionary level within the community, to bring home our daughters and sons, and sisters and brothers, fathers and mothers and welcome them home with love and a new revolutionary comradeship of unity.

13. To take control of all state land and that of the capitalist class and to give back the land to the people. To form laws and codes that safeguard that no person can own the land, or sell the land, but rather the nations' people own the land and use it for their needs and interest to live. No one can own or sell the air, the sky, the water, the trees, the birds, the sun, for all of this world belongs to the people of this earth.

14. To take controls of all buildings and apartment buildings of the capitalist class and fascist government and then to totally destroy the rent system of exploitation.

15. To build a federation of nations, who shall formulate

programs and unions of actions and interests that will destroy the capitalist value system and its other anti-human institutions and who will be able to do this by meeting all the basic needs of all of the people and their nations. For they will be all able to do this because each nation will have full control of all of its industries and institutions and does not run them for profit, but in the full interest of all the people of its nation.

16. To destroy all forms and institutions of Racism, Sexism, Ageism, Capitalism, Fascism, Individualism, Possessiveness, Competiveness and all other such institutions that have made and sustained capitalism and the capitalist class system that has oppressed and exploitated all of the people of our history.

By this means and the mutual aid and unity of each nation within The Symbionese Federation, will each nation be able to provide to each person and couple and family free of cost the five basic needs of life, which are food, health care, housing, education and clothing, and in this way allowing people to be able to find and form new values and new systems of relationships and interests based on a new meaning to life and love.

IF THE QUEST FOR FREEDOM IS DEATH
THEN BY THE DEATH OF THE ENEMY WILL
BLACK AND OTHER OPPRESSED PEOPLE
FIND AND REGAIN THEIR FREEDOM

THE TERMS OF THE WAR COUNCIL

UNDATED

THE UNITED SYMBIONESE WAR COUNCIL
TERMS OF MILITARY/POLITICAL ALLIANCE

Our commitment to the revolutionary struggle for self-determination for all oppressed people and races and the international proletarian revolution is total and fully uncompromisable. Therefore, any relationship the Symbionese War Council has with any group or organization is based on their active military/political commitment to the goal of gaining freedom for all oppressed people and races.

1. Our alliance with any group or organization is based upon their firm decision to fight as well as talk in behalf of the people's interest, and once this commitment is clear then we can come together in order to:

1) collectively develop a common strategy

2) work together to develop tactical co-ordination

3) Assist each other in developing the abilities and talents of all the members of the Symbionese War Council and to analyze the strengths and weaknesses of the leadership in order to constantly better all aspects of the ability and actions of the War Council, and its individual leadership from other organizations.

2. Command positions of The War Council are subject to

the approval of all members of the council, based upon the military/political thinking and ability of the presented officer to work with others in the interest of freedom for all people and races.

3. Command positions in The War Council are not appointed by one who knows, ones sex, ones color or the group or organization one belongs to, but only by ones Courage, Determination, Intelligence, Aggressive Initiative and Capability as a leader, and ones Military/Political thinking.

4. All members of The War Council are expected and fully are responsible for the military political leadership of The S.L.A., they must fight and speak for the people and this must be understood clearly by all members.

5. No member of The War Council can elect or select himself or herself to a position such as the head of a government or people's council; the War Council is totally an alliance OF WAR AGAINST THE COMMON ENEMY. The people themselves shall have and hold the ONLY RIGHT to select and elect their governments and government heads of state.

6. It is NOT the policy of The War Council to rip off leadership or membership from other organizations, but rather it is the policy of The War Council to aid and support the development and education of leadership to fullfill truly its responsibility to the people, and to allow the collective intelligence, leadership and resourcefullness of the leadership from different organizations and groups to flourish together and grow together; thereby forming an area where the collective interests and needs as well as weaknesses and strengths of each can benefit each IN THE COMMON STRUGGLE TO LIQUIDATE THE

COMMON ENEMY.

7. A successful military force is a necessity for actualizing political goals and must therefore be held as a priority; therefore, the true assistance in the supplying of military equipment, materials, finances, personal is of the utmost importance, once these forces have fully committed themselves to open and total warfare against the common enemy and members of The War Council must understand this clearly.

8. Leadership of any group or organization who is truly committed and in agreement with the goals of the S.L.A. and the terms of military/political alliance may be presented to The War Council; however, the presented officer's membership is not confirmed until it is verified that prior to presentation for membership a combat action has been taken part in by that group or organization within the last 12 months.

9. Once The War Council collectively agrees to an action or plan of strategy then that action shall be understood as an action of the S.L.A., and not of any single group or organization. Just as the fingers cannot call themselves a fist, and the fist cannot call itself the fingers. From time to time the membership on the War Council may disagree upon a particular action or strategy. When in disagreement, that particular membership need not participate in The S.L.A. action, but membership on The War Council is maintained only as long as all commitments made to the collective Symbionese War Council are continued to be fully adhered to. It is the disagreeing group or organization's responsibility to, on its own, prove out their ideas in order to change or modify its own or the collective War Council's direction.

10. It is the policy of The War Council not to involve itself

in the internal political affairs or disagreements that may result within different organizations or groups. However, The War Council recognizes and accepts membership to the Council of any military/political unit, cell or organization that qualifies and shall recognize them as true representatives of that particular organization or group. It is the collective policy of The War Council that the failure of the elected leadership to take her or his revolutionary responsibility as far as the War Council is concerned shall be totally the responsibility of the elected leader and not that of The War Council.

11. Organizations or groups that wish to serve in combat units must select two persons, one female and one male (if possible), who have full responsibility and authority to act and represent their group or organization and who will hold a command position in the unified command of The United Symbionese War Council.

12. All members of The Symbionese War Council must clearly understand that our commitment is total and our goal is the total freedom of the people and children and the destroying totally of the common enemy. Therefore, it is held that any restraining of supplies or other war materials etc. for political reasons or reactionary reasons or political chess games with the enemy, by any officer or other persons in the War Council, that by its actions endangers the lives of the women and men of The Symbionese Liberation Army shall be held as a full and total violation of this alliance pact and compromising with the enemy and the freedom and life of the people and children and therefore is punishable by death.

TO THOSE WHO WOULD BEAR
THE HOPES AND FUTURE OF THE PEOPLE
LET THE VOICE OF THEIR GUNS
EXPRESS THE WORDS OF FREEDOM.

Gen. Field Marshall
CIN
S.L.A.

DESTROY THE ENEMY AND FREE THE PEOPLE

UNDATED

TACTICAL SUPPORT UNITS

Each cell of The S.L.A. TACTICAL SUPPORT UNITS is composed of elements of other organizations and groups and individuals. Under the strategy of The S.L.A. it is totally impossible to follow the egotistic aspirations of many leaders of political organizations, since they continue to organize new organizations everytime one falls apart, when they fail to understand that the people always organize to fight the enemy; and when leaders fail to start the fight, then the people fall from that organization.

To continue in this manner is totally reactionary, egotistic, opportunist and anti-revolutionary, since to do so only allows for the continued grouping and regrouping of the same revolutionary people for the fight that never comes and with the only purpose of organizing.

This is totally anti-revolutionary for within the true purpose of revolution there is only TWO DEEP PURPOSES: TO DESTROY THE ENEMY AND FREE THE PEOPLE. This in itself means the need for an army of the people that fights the enemy.

In order to organize, one must organize in support of something, one does not organize in support of having or belonging to or just to organize, but rather one must have a purpose to organize around, and since in revolution it is the purpose to organize to fight the enemy and to support those that fight on the front lines, it is then clear that the people organize to fight and destroy the enemy. They do not organize to fight the enemy and then when it comes time to fight, claim that to fight the enemy will endanger the organization for this would show them to be lovers of positions and the organization and not true revolutionaries that love the people and children.

Since you as members of the people have organized to fight the enemy, for the reason that you are and do love the people, then it is clear to you where your true responsibility is, and that is to join and support those who are in the front lines fighting the enemy of us all, regardless of what color, group or organization they belong to, for the people are just this, they are not an organization or color or group, they are the oppressed, exploitated and the murdered, they are those we love and for whom we, if needed, are willing to die for, they are our children.

Therefore what is needed now is for you as lovers of the people to select in what area you are able and willing to fight in or give support to, either in the combat units or support units of The S.L.A., the choice is yours alone: to be and show yourselves as lovers of the people and our children and true to your word revolutionaries, or as egotistic opportunists and lovers of the group and organization and enemies of the people.

MOBILITY UNIT

It is the responsibility of the Mobility Unit to provide for the movement of supplies and military personal and the necessary equipment needed to safely move said personal and supplies. It is responsible for the safe movement of supplies between other units and to and from the combat units, and providing needed hiding places and disguises necessary in the movement of combat elements, and supplies and equipment. It is also responsible for receiving and decentralized stocking of those supplies and equipment under it's authority and which combat forces have found to be in excess of their supplies after expropriation operations.

1. The building of hideouts that will serve from time to time the needs of combat units in operations in different area's of the state and other states as actions allow.

2. The acquiring, building and camouflaging of vans, buses, and other means to allow safe movement of supplies and personal.

3. Arming and armor plating of said type autos and the building of means of concealment for supplies and personal, to also build defense systems into said autos, such as oil, smoke, and nail release systems.

4. Maintaining of autos in top condition and giving them top speed and drive ability at the same time bulletproof and tires ect.

5. Acquiring, decentralized stocking and receiving and providing of phony and real ID papers, uniforms of movement, such as disguises for mailmen, priest, gas man, policemen, nun, army, navy, airforce, wigs, shoes and type said equipment, parts to repair autos, gas and oil facilities, tires, and power generating equipment for tools.

MEDICAL UNIT

It is the responsibility of the Medical Unit to provide medical combat personal when combat units open operations in any area of the state. To provide needed medical care that elements of our forces may need from time to time and to decentralize stocking of medical supplies and equipment under its authority and that may be sent from forward combat troops after expropriation operations against the enemy. It is the Medical Units responsibility to build and find means to safely hide medical equipment. . . . It is the responsibility of the Medical Unit to build and provide underground operating rooms and the needed personal and equipment to run them in all and different areas of the state, both in urban and rural areas.

1. The building of recuperation areas that are security sound.

2. The building of mobile medical teams that are able to be within a 15 mile area from force units in it's operations thereby allowing combat elements aid as soon as possible under war conditions.

3. The building of training facility for medical combat training, warfare and it's medical needs call for military medical training in the areas of gun shot wounds, cuts, shock, gas burns, poison ect. and should be held as the main training priority.

4. Acquiring of generating power equipment for operating rooms and medical equipment.

5. The acquiring, receiving and decentralized stockpiling of medical supplies and equipment across the state in safe and underground areas with only a few security cleared personal knowing the whereabouts of said supplies.

ARMORMENT UNIT

It is the responsibility of the Armorment Unit to provide, stock, build and repair military equipment and to develop new revolutionary weapons. To provide decentralized stocking and hiding areas for weapons and ammo and other type equipment, and supply combat elements with supplies when needed.

1. To build booby traps, bulletproofing, and mines, electric shotgun mines ect.

2. To build facilities for the making of machine guns, reloading equipment, cyanide bombs and bullets, poison and arms to fire them with.

3. Acquiring or building ammo, gas masks, sniper rifles, silencers, mortars, anti-tank weapons, flamethrowers, and explosives.

4. To work with others in the use of the people and the people's creativity to find new means and ways to destroy the enemy better than he can destroy us.

PROVISION UNIT

It is the responsibility of the Provision Unit to provide food and other such supplies as are under it's authority to those units that request it, to see to it that the needs of the Medical Unit are met and that of other units. To form and develop hiding places and underground areas where food and other provisions can be safely stored.

1. Stocking of canned foods and other foods and acquiring of means to maintain the food value of these foods.

2. Decentralized stocking across the state of foods, cooking fuels, equipment for cooking, soap and other equipment necessary.

COMMUNICATION UNIT

It is the responsibility of the Communication Unit to see to it and provide all combat support groups, support units and command sections with communication equipment, to repair said and build it's own equipment if possible to train personal in the use of radio and type equipment and to provide trained personal to combat units and command sections.

1. To build and maintain jamming and monitoring equipment and personal to jam and monitor enemy communications.

2. To build with other units, communication lines between other units, by clear and approved security means, to form teams of communications runners, made up of dogs, birds, women, children, old comrade people, ect., to form areas to aid units in forming dead drops and end cuts for security.

3. To maintain, acquire and receive equipment that has been expropriated by combat units from the enemy, and supply said equipment when needed to other units.

4. To stock by decentralized means across the state these supplies and to also build and set up communication teams across the state with both long and short range radio equipment, thereby giving them the ability to keep all of our units in full contact with each at all times.

INTELLIGENCE UNIT

It is the responsibility of the Intelligence Unit to build and provide means whereby the enemy is always two steps behind us, but never in front of us, it must maintain a ever flowing line of information on the enemy, informers, and supplies that our forces may need. It must intake intelligence and find out clearly the truth of it and pass it on to command sections as soon as possible, it must not overlook any action of the enemy or those who are near the enemy. It must maintain running files and run photo teams to be able to supply the unit and central command with all possible information on the enemy or buildings and terrain that may be needed in carrying out of operations.

1. Building of files on known informers and agents, addresses, family, photo if possible, car color and license number.

2. The forming of information on the movements of police, agents, prison officers and family, photos if possible.

3. Formulating information on movement of money, military equipment, medical supplies, food supplies, arms, explosives, radio equipment, gas and oil and other type supplies.

4. Acquiring of maps of government institutions, jails, prisons, banks, storm drains, communication stations and lines, power plants and lines, oil and gas and other fuel supply tanks areas, airports, navy, army base area and explosive and arms makers locations and security that is used for all these type buildings and areas.

5. Information on movements of police and other military elements, placing of S.L.A. agents in police and military institutions.

6. Forming of counter intelligence agent teams and the forming of means to carry out security checks of S.L.A. personal.

PROPAGANDA UNIT

It is the responsibility of the Propaganda Unit to maintain clandestine press and printing equipment, mimeograph equipment or other type means to provide newspapers, pamphlets, flyers and stamps for propaganda and agitation against the enemy and to allow the people to know both our victories and our failures, to provide the people with truthful information on it's oppression and the need for them to fight against the common enemy as one people.

1. The incorporation of members of the people for the purpose of working in propaganda actions in their community, to train them in the use of walls, tape recordings, loudspeakers, drawings and other forms of propaganda.

2. To provide propaganda to the actions of combat units against the enemy, to seek to turn enemy soldiers against their officers, to seek to keep unity among our people, while the enemy is trying to divide us.

3. To use radio and other means to bring forth a war of nerves against the enemy, and to give the spirit of struggle to all our people.

4. To by letters sent to government officers attempt to turn them to our side and explaining the meaning of our armed forces actions and that their only hope is to take the side that will win in the end, the people.

5. The misinforming, spreading lies and forming of un-

certainty in the enemies forces and personal in local areas, announcing of false information to the enemy, using rumors, information on corruption of government members and all possible means to bring about a war of nerves upon the enemy.

THE LIQUIDATION OF THE COMMON ENEMY

AUGUST 21, 1973

THE SYMBIONESE FEDERATION AND THE SYMBIONESE LIBERATION ARMY

DECLARATION OF REVOLUTIONARY WAR AND THE SYMBIONESE PROGRAM

August 21, 1973

The Symbionese Federation and The Symbionese Liberation Army is a united and federated grouping of members of different races and people and socialist political parties of the oppressed people of The Fascist United States of America, who have under black and minority leadership formed and joined The Symbionese Federated Republic and have agreed to struggle together in behalf of all their people and races and political parties' interest in the gaining of FREEDOM and SELF DETERMINATION and INDEPENDANCE for all their people and races.

The Symbionese Federation is NOT A GOVERNMENT, but rather it is a united and federated formation of members of different races and people and political parties who have agreed to struggle in a UNITED FRONT for the independence and self determination of each of their races and people and The Liquidation of the Common Enemy.

And who by this federated formation represent their future and independent pre-governments and nations of their people and races. The Symbionese Federation is NOT A PARTY, but rather is a Federation, for its members are made up of members of all political parties and organizations and races of all the most oppressed people of this fascist nation, thereby forming unity and the full representation of the interests of all people.

The Symbionese Liberation Army is an army of the people, and is made up of members of all the people. The S.L.A. has no political power or political person over it that dictates who will fight and die if needed for the freedom of our people and children, but does not risk their life or fight too for our freedom, but rather the S.L.A. is both political and military in that in the S.L.A. the army officer, whether female or male, is also the political officer and they both are the daughters and sons of the people and they both fight as well as speak for the freedom of our people and children.

The Symbionese Federation and The Symbionese Liberation Army is made up of the aged, youth and women and men of all races and people. The name Symbionese is taken from the word symbiosis and we define its meaning as a body of dissimilar bodies and organisms living in deep and loving harmony and partnership in the best interest of all within the body.

We of the Symbionese Federation and The S.L.A. define ourselves by this name because it states that we are no longer willing to allow the enemy of all our people and children to murder, oppress and exploit us nor define us by color and thereby maintain division among us, but rather have joined together under black and minority leadership in behalf of all our different races and people to build a better and new world for our children and people's future. We are a United Front and Federated Coalition of members from the Asian, Black, Brown, Indian, White, Women, Grey and Gay Liberation Movements.

Who have all come to see and understand that only if we unite and build our new world and future, will there really be a future for our children and people. We of the People and not the ruling capitalist class, will build a new world and system. Where there is really freedom and a true meaning to justice and equality for all women and men of all races and people, and an end to the murder and oppression, exploitation of all people.

We of the Symbionese Federation and The S.L.A. are the children of all oppressed people, who have decided to redefine ourselves as a Symbionese Race and People. Yet, recognizing the rich cultures of each and enforcing our rights to existance of our many cultures within a united federation of independant and sovereign nations, each of them flourishing and protected by its own laws and codes of self determination.

We are of many colors, but yet of one mind, for we all in history's time on this earth have become part of each other in suffering and in mind, and have agreed that the murder, oppression, and exploitation of our children and people must end now, for we all have seen the murder, oppression and exploitation of our people for too long under the hand of the same enemy and class of people and under the same system.

Knowing this, the Symbionese Federation and The S.L.A. know that our often murderous alienation from each other aids and is one of the fundamental strengths behind the ruling capitalist class's ability to murder and oppress us all. By not allowing them to define us by color, and also recognizing that by refusing ourselves to also internalize this false division definition, knowing that in mind and body we are facing the same enemy and that we are all comrades of one people, the murdered and oppressed, we are now able to become a united people under the Symbionese Federation and make true the words of our codes of unity that TO DIE A RACE, AND BE BORN A NATION, IS TO BECOME FREE.

Therefore, we of the Symbionese Federation and The S.L.A. DO NOT under the rights of human beings submit to the murder, oppression and exploitation of our children and people and do under the rights granted to the people under The Declaration of Independance of The United States, do now by the rights of our children and people and by Force of Arms and with every drop of our blood, *Declare Revolutionary War* against The Fascist Capitalist Class, and all their agents of murder, oppression and exploitation. We support by Force of Arms the just struggles of all oppressed people for self determination and independance within the United States and The World. And hereby offer to all liberation movements, revolutionary workers groups, and peoples organizations our total aid and support for the struggle for freedom and justice for all people and races. We call upon all revolutionary black and other oppressed people within the Fascist United States to come together and join The Symbionese Federation and fight in the forces of The Symbionese Liberation Army.

October 19, 1973

A woman is slashed to death and her husband is viciously beaten in the Telegraph Hill area of San Francisco – the beginning of the "Zebra" killings. Targeting whites exclusively, the killers – four black Muslims who worked together at a moving company – murdered at least fifteen people and wounded eight more until their arrests on May 1, 1974, and convictions almost two years later.

November 1, 1973

At 10:30 p.m., three white Emeryville policemen pursue, shoot, and kill unarmed fourteen-year-old African-American Tyrone Guyton; no indictments are issued against the police officers.

November 6, 1973

Leaving his office, Superintendent Marcus Foster of the Oakland Board of Education (the first African American to hold the office) is shot to death by the Symbionese Liberation Army; his friend, Deputy Superintendent Robert Blackburn, is seriously wounded. The bullets are tipped with cyanide. According to later testimony, Patricia Mizmoon Soltysik and Nancy Ling Perry shot Foster, and Donald DeFreeze shotgunned Blackburn; Joseph Remiro and Russell Little were in a nearby getaway car.

THE ASSASSINATION OF DR. MARCUS FOSTER

NOVEMBER 6, 1973

SYMBIONESE LIBERATION ARMY
WESTERN REGIONAL YOUTH UNIT

Communique No. 1

Subject: The Board of Education

The Implementation of the Internal Warfare Identification Computer System

Warrant Order: Execution by Cyanide Bullets

Date: November 6, 1973

Warrant Issued By: The Court of the People

Charges: Supporting and taking part in the forming and implementation of a Political Police Force operating within the Schools of the People.

Supporting and taking part in the forming and implementation of Bio-Dossiers through The Forced Youth Identification Program.

Supporting and taking part in the building of composite files for the Internal Warfare Identification Computer System.

Target: Dr. Marcus A. Foster, Superintendent of Schools, Oakland, California

Robert Blackburn, Deputy Superintendent, Oakland, California

On the afore stated date, elements of the United Federated Forces of The S.L.A. did attack the Fascist Board of Education, Oakland, California, through the person of Dr. Marcus A. Foster, Superintendent of Schools, and Robert Blackburn, Deputy Superintendent.

This attack is to serve notice on the Board of Education and its fascist elements that they have come to the attention of The S.L.A. and The Court of the People and have been found guilty of supporting and taking part in crimes committed against the children and the life of the people.

This attack is also to serve notice on the fascist Board of Education and its fascist supporters that The Court of the People have issued a Death Warrant on All Members and Supporters of the Internal Warfare Identification Computer System. This SHOOT ON SIGHT order will stay in effect until such time as ALL POLITICAL POLICE ARE REMOVED FROM OUR SCHOOLS AND ALL PHOTO AND OTHER FORMS OF IDENTIFICATION ARE STOPPED.

Indictment:

No. 1: The Board of Education has taken upon itself the role of forming and supporting a Special Political Police Force to occupy and patrol the schools in our cities. The vast Black, Chicano, Asian and conscious White youth communities of the Oakland-Berkeley area understand that this newest extension of police surveilance is patterned after fascist Amerikan tactics of genocide, murder and imprisonment practiced by Amerikan financed puppet governments in Vietnam, The Philippines, Chile and South Africa. We recognize that the school system censors and controls what we read, and that the Special Political Police Force is to censor and control what we say and do.

No. 2: The Board of Education has taken upon itself the role of forming and supporting the implementation of Bio-Dossiers through the Forced Youth Identification Program. The Photo Identification Program, with the addition of composite files, is patterned after the system of apartheid in South Africa. The Bio-Dossiers classify our youth according to color and "criminal tendencies" (will to be free) and seek to eliminate all our valiant freedom fighters by "relocating" (incarcerating) them to such concentration camps as Tehachapi Prison. Under the Preventative Crime Act such concentration camps have the authority to incarcerate our youth from age of 15 for an "indefinite" period of time. The Preventative Crime Act stipulates that any youth displaying violent or "crimminal" potential or the possibility of violent or "crimminal" potential in the future, in other words, any youth who oppose the current system of censored Political Police-State education and seek to organize against it are to be classified as dangerous and either disarmed, shot or imprisoned for expressing their rights to be free, and defending the rights to freedom of their fellow brothers and sisters.

No. 3: The Board of Education has taken upon itself the role of supporting and taking part in the implementation of the Internal Warfare Identification Computer System. The Internal Warfare tapes are based in the FBI's master computer system. Each state is required to feed this main computer with information from the composite files of individuals who have expressed political views that may be regarded as differing from those of the fascist ruling class. Members of liberation movements and organizations, as well as single individuals, are identified through photographs and bio-dossiers supplied, in the case of our youth, by the Boards of Education and Public School Systems in our cities. The racist nature of the Internal Warfare Identification Computer System is clear since blacks and other minorities who refuse to serve the rich ruling class are automatically classified as potentially violent and "crimminal." The CIA-ITT financed junto government in Chile uses similar bio-dossiers to murder all identified people who oppose the military take over there or who do not serve and support the interests of the wealthy. Similar programs are carried out by governments financed by Amerika and its military corporate enterprises throughout the world in the lands of the robbed; Vietnam, The Philippines, Chile, Brazil, Uruguay, South Africa are some prime examples.

The Black, Chicano, Asian and conscious White youth in our communities recognize the importance of the Oakland-Berkeley area to the liberation struggle of all oppressed people. We know that the ruling class must seek to stop the revolutionary community here before the ruling class can regain its arm of control around the struggling and oppressed people of the world.

We understand that the definition of a fascist government necessitates the elimination of all who oppose its controls. We know that the school system does not educate us, but rather it lies to us in an attempt to perpetuate the interests of the rich ruling class. News of the successful liberation struggles of our brothers and sisters throughout the world is stifled because the enemy fears our knowledge of the fact that a truly determined people can never be defeated. We reject totally the ruling class values of personal material gain and competition among ourselves and we know that the enemy fears our understanding of the fact that nothing is more precious than freedom. The myth of a high-style superfly life and fashion show (a capitalistic rip-off) does not sway us for we know that the fascist government of Amerika supplies the dope and the clothes and wants us to spend the rest of our lives paying for them. We are well aware that a fascist government will allow some of us to get high, while the rest of us go to concentration camps, and none of us are free.

It is clear that Dr. Foster and sideman, deputy superintendent Robert Blackburn, represent the rich ruling class and big business, and not the children and youth of our communities. The school system which they represent and serve does not teach us or address itself to the needs of our survival, but rather it does perpetuate the values of big business and the wealthy. Under the current system, the ruling class is educated to exploit, and our children and youth are educated to serve. We are not deceived by the superintendent and deputy. Robert Blackburn is a former director of education for the Peace Corps in East Africa. The Peace Corps, as well as AID, are promoted and financed as a front for the CIA, and have long been arms of Amerika imperialist and racist oppression and genocide. Dr. Foster is a former member of the Philadelphia Crime Commission, and now his advancement within the fascist process found him as initiator, promoter and supporter of Political Police Units armed with riot shotguns, to patrol our schools.

The Oakland-Berkeley area is considered potentially dangerous to Amerikan ruling class, that is why it has been selected for the Political Police Force Within the Schools and the Forced Youth Identification Program. Let it be known to those who sign for the implementation of these fascist programs, that the death of our manchild comrade youth, 14-year-old Tyrone Guyton, murdered on November 1st by three goons from the Emeryville Political Police Patrol, is NOT FORGOTTEN. Tyrone fell victim to the racist enemy who is instituting programs such as those initiated by Marcus Foster and Robert Blackburn aimed at the control, imprisonment, execution and genocide of blacks and other minorities. Let it be known to those who sign for the implementation of these fascist programs, that they sign their own death warrants. We of the black and other revolutionary youth communities have for too long seen the enemy prostitute our mothers, imprison our fathers, shoot our brothers and sterilize our sisters. We have learned from these lessons; therefore, notice is hereby served on the enemy political police state and all its lackeys that we hold as an example to follow the courage of our slain comrade-in-arms Jonathan Jackson and we call upon our mothers, fathers, sisters and brothers saying TO THOSE WHO WOULD BEAR THE HOPES AND FUTURE OF OUR PEOPLE, LET THE VOICE OF THEIR GUNS EXPRESS THE WORDS OF FREEDOM.

"DEATH TO THE FASCIST INSECT
THAT PREYS UPON THE LIFE
OF THE PEOPLE"

S.L.A.

THE WARRANT IS RESCINDED

NOVEMBER 15, 1973

SYMBIONESE LIBERATION ARMY
WESTERN REGIONAL YOUTH UNIT

Communique No. 2
Subject: The Board of Education
The Respecting of the Rights and Wishes of the People
Notification: Court Order
Date: November 15, 1973
Order Issued By: The Court of the People

It has come to the attention of The Symbionese Liberation Army and The Court of the People that the fascist Board of Education has made an attempt to heed and respect the rights and wishes of the people by stating that they will not continue to take part in crimes committed against the children and the life of the people. Therefore, it is the decision of this court that the SHOOT ON SIGHT warrant issued November 6, 1973, be rescinded, and that all forces of the S.L.A. and the People's Army halt their attack on this aspect of the fascist enemy state. However, in the event that the fascist Board of Education does attempt to disguise their intentions and at any time reinstates programs of Political Police Forces in our schools, Forced Youth Identification cards, and contributions to the Internal Warfare Identification Computer System, then the Death Warrant Order is to be immediately re-activated without warning.

The Forces of The Symbionese Liberation Army commend the people for their courage in refusing to fall prey to offers of bribery and rewards to be given for information which the enemy will then use against the defenders of the people. We praise the spirit, determination and strength of the vast Black, Chicano, Asian and conscious white communities of the Oakland-Berkeley area, and remind the enemy rich ruling class that the people will always understand the effectiveness and tactics of revolutionary justice, and will never be deceived by the distortions and lies of the fascist news media. Marcus Foster has been likened to one of our slain leaders. We ask, who has ever heard of a Martin Luther King on the Philadelphia Crime Commission? Who has ever heard of a Martin Luther King having an aide who is a CIA agent, formerly acting as director of education for the Peace Corps in East Africa? We are all well aware that the fascist news media seeks to condition us by repressing the truth.

The people have seen no evidence to indicate that Deputy Superintendent Blackburn is in fact still alive. Traditionally, the fascist news media is quick to display photographs of members of the enemy state who have managed to survive revolutionary justice and the will of the people. Usually we would see the enemy as he lays in his plush, private hospital room, while the wounds of all oppressed people remain unattended. However, if Blackburn is alive, The Symbionese Liberation Army and The Court of the People wish to point out the contradiction between the medical care received by those who represent the rich ruling class, and that received by members of the poor and oppressed communities. It is obvious that medical technology does exist and that is a question of who receives the benefits of such care? Tyrone Guyton was shot down, handcuffed, and allowed to bleed to death in the gutter. For too long we have seen our people die from the enemy's bullets.

"DEATH TO THE FASCIST INSECT THAT PREYS UPON THE LIFE OF THE PEOPLE."

December 19, 1973

The San Francisco *Chronicle* and *Examiner* publish articles announcing the engagement of Patricia Campbell Hearst to Steven Andrew Weed. The *Chronicle* notes that Hearst is enrolled at UC Berkeley as an art history major. After reading the articles, SLA member William Harris looks up Hearst's home address in a student directory at the university.

January 10, 1974

Russell Little and Joseph Remiro are arrested after getting lost on their way to the SLA safehouse at 1560 Sutherland Court in Concord, California; attempting to escape the police, Little is wounded in the shoulder and captured immediately, and Remiro is caught four hours later. One of the weapons found on Little and Remiro had been used in the murder of Dr. Foster.

Nancy Ling Perry attempts to burn down the Sutherland Court safehouse; due to a lack of oxygen, the fire is small and nearly extinguishes itself before firemen arrive. Inside the house police discover ammunition, stolen license plates and library books, bomb-making matériel, and a treasure trove of SLA documents. One of the documents is a "target" list; included on the list is "Patricia Campbell Hearst, nineteen years old; daughter of Randolph and Catherine Hearst – *arrest warrant issued.*"

MY TRUE NAME IS FAHIZAH

JANUARY 17, 1974

[transcript of audio tape]

the voice of Donald DeFreeze (Cinque)

To those who would bear the hopes and future of our people, let the voice of their guns express the words of freedom.

the voice of Nancy Ling Perry (Fahizah)

Greetings, my comrade sisters and brothers, all love, power, and freedom to you. I am very glad to have this opportunity to speak to you, even though I know that what I am feeling cannot be completely expressed in words. You may have heard of me, not because I am any more important than any of you, but simply because my former name has been in the news lately. My name was Nancy Ling Perry, but my true name is Fahizah. What that name means is one who is victorious, and I am one who believes in the liberation and victory of the people, because I have learned that what one really believes in is what will come to pass. So, my name is Fahizah and I am a freedom fighter in an information/intelligence unit of the United Federated Forces of the Symbionese Liberation Army. I still am that, in spite of the fact that I am now being sought for a political action, and in spite of the fact that two of my closest compañeros are now chained in the Adjustment Center, the prisoner's prison, at San Quentin concentration camp. It was reported that I have been unsuccessfully begging for money. That's a lie. If I needed money I would appropriate it. Another lie was reported saying that I am hiding out with Venceremos political group, but I don't hide out with any political organization. I am still with other members of the SLA information/intelligence unit, and I am hiding only from the enemy and not from the people. I have no intention of deserting my commitment nor would I ever try to run away from it, because I have learned that there is no flight to freedom except that of an armed projectile. Although it is the practice of the Symbionese Liberation Army to act rather than talk, I am compelled to speak because I wish to make clear my position, why I am fighting, and what it is that I am fighting for, what the purpose and nature of the SLA information/intelligence unit is, and why I will continue to fight.

First of all, I think I should tell you something about my background and the evolution of my consciousness. Basically, I have three backgrounds: I have a work background, a love background, and a prison background. My prison background means that I have close ties and feelings with our incarcerated brothers and sisters. What they have taught me is that if people on the outside do not understand the necessity of defending them through force of arms, then it is because these people on the outside do not yet realize that they are in an immediate danger of being thrown into concentration camps themselves, tortured, or shot down in the streets for expressing their beliefs. What my love background taught me was a whole lot of what love is all about, and that the greater one's capacity for love is, the greater is one's longing for freedom. What my high school background taught me is that one of the things that every revolutionary does is to fight to get back the fruits of her or his own labor and the control of his or her own destiny.

When I was in high school in 1963–64, I witnessed the first military coup against we the people of this country. I saw us passively sit by our TVs and unconsciously watch as the militarily-armed corporate state took over the existing government and blatantly destroyed the Constitution that some of us still believed in. I listened to the people around me deny that a military coup had taken place and claim that such a thing could not happen here. The people that I grew up around were so politically naive that their conceptions of a military coup only recognized those that have occurred in South America and African countries where the military and ruling class took over the government by an open force of arms. But the method of taking over the government was different here. Here the coup was simply accomplished by assassinating the then-President John Kennedy, and then assassinating any further opposition to the dictator who was to take power. That dictator is the current President Richard Nixon. In 1964, I witnessed these and other somewhat hidden beginnings of the military/corporate state which we now live in, and I heard my teachers and the government-controlled media spread lies about what had happened. I saw the civil rights protests, the killings and bombings of my black sisters and brothers, and the conditioned reactions of extreme racism in my school and home. When I questioned my teachers about how these occurrences related to the meanings of democracy and freedom that we were told existed to protect us all, the answer I got was that we were better off not knowing the truth about what was happening. I told my teachers and my family and my friends that I felt that we were all being used as pawns and puppets, and that those who had taken over the government were trying to keep us asleep and in a political stupor. I asked my teachers to tell me what happened in Nazi Germany. I asked them to tell me the meaning of fascism. I asked them to tell me the meaning of genocide. And when I began to hear about a war in Vietnam, I asked them to tell me the meaning of imperialism. The answer to all my questions was either silence, or a reply filled with confusion and lies, and a racist pride and attitude that said well, after all, it was all for us.

The experience of living in America has since taught me the realities of what fascism, imperialism, and genocide mean, and I have discovered the truth about the military takeover and the police state dictatorship, not because I studied about it in college, but because I see it every day, and because truth is something that is honestly known, as easily as beauty is seen. There is no need for me to relate here everything that I have seen, or everything that I am sure you are already aware of. I am sure, my sisters and brothers, that you realize that the government is now in the rapid and steady process of removing the means of survival from the lower class and giving these benefits to the middle class in an effort to rally support from them. And as the government is removing these means of survival from the people, then naturally the people who have been robbed must in turn take back what rightfully belongs to them, and take back what they need in order to survive. This the current dictatorship calls a crime, whether the people take food from the grocery store, or take to the streets to make a speech, or take a gun in their hand to defend themselves.

As a member of the Symbionese Liberation Army information/intelligence unit, I fight against our common oppressor, and this I do with my gun as well as my mind. I try to use my mind and my imagination to uncover facts, so that when the SLA attacks it will be in the right place, and that the actions of the more experienced SLA combat units will truly serve to benefit the people and answer their needs. The action taken by the SLA combat unit in reference to the Oakland Board of Education was a specific response to political police state programs and the failure of the Board to heed the rights and demands of the people in the community. The specific programs was one of the photo identification, similar to the system of apartheid in South Africa, biological classification in the form of bio-dossiers which classify students according to race and political beliefs, internal warfare computer files, and armed police-state patrols within the schools. Intensely thorough intelligence operations carried out by the SLA information unit were able to obtain factual information that Foster's signature was the first to appear on the Nixon Administration-inspired proposal for armed police agents within certain Oakland schools and various forms of computer classification of students. Further intelligence revealed that Foster's background included membership on the Philadelphia Crime Commission. Foster's sideman, Blackburn, is a CIA agent. As director of education in East Africa he worked to implement test programs against black people there, and he trained other agents to carry them out so that he could return to this country and introduce those same programs here. I feel a need to explain this again because I want to make it clear that the SLA was not indiscriminantly issuing death warrants for Foster, Blackburn or anyone else, but rather we were attacking the programs and proposals of which they were the initiators, supporters, and first signers. Such an attack was the only means left open to us to demand that the people's wishes be met, and that all such dangerous, genocidal programs be stopped.

The regime-controlled media has made some reference to the effect that this action was carried out by white people made up in blackface. Members of the SLA do not have to make up in blackface in order to defend the black community, since the SLA is a federation formed in the style of a revolutionary United Nations whose commanding leadership is composed of representatives of the black, brown, yellow, red, and white communities. We have more than enough members from every race to carry out any operation. As revolutionaries we would never disguise ourselves by race, because we would never deliberately act in a manner that would bring further police investigation onto any one race of peoples. But I would like to ask, since when does one have to be black in order to care about the murder of fourteen-year-old Tyrone Guyton by political police-state death squads, since when does one have to be white in order to feel for the starving children in Appalachia, since when does one have to be Asian in order to care about stopping the napalming of children in Vietnam, since when does one have to be brown in order to fight against the mass slaughters being conducted by the military junta in Chile? Since when? Not since we have come to realize that we are all one in struggle.

I am a member of the Symbionese Liberation Army information/intelligence unit, and that means that my responsibility is to aid the combat units with information, and keep myself armed at all times. I am in a race to learn how to fight, because I am in a race to survive. SLA information/intelligence units have a military/political alliance with SLA combat units. What that means is that information units totally support armed struggle. That is to say that all members of the SLA understand that politics cannot be separated from struggle, in fact politics have no meaning without armed information and combat units to give politics a purpose.

The Symbionese Liberation Army is unlike many existing political organizations in this country which support the armed liberation struggles of peoples throughout the world, but when it comes to the struggle here in America, they consistently denounce militancy and revolutionary violence, and in so doing denounce the only means left to the people to achieve their liberation. I believe that whenever people are confronted with oppression, starvation, and the death of their freedom that they want to fight. It has been the history of many political leaders to suppress this will of the people, and to pretend that the people do not have the right to fight, and to pretend that the people will somehow achieve their liberation without revolutionary violence. But the truth is that there has never been a precedent for a nonviolent revolution; the defenseless and unarmed people of Chile can testify to that. All members of the SLA recognize that we, right here in America, are in a state of war, and that in a state of war, all must be armed and understand the true meaning of self-defense. When any member of the people's army strikes out at the murderer of our people and children, we are doing so in self-defense, we are doing so because we are left no alternative, and force of arms is now our only legal means to effect revolutionary justice. However, the natural instincts of many people in our country have become perverted by the conditionings to which we have been subjected, they have been conditioned to be afraid of revolutionary violence. I no longer have these fears because as a comrade of mine, Osceola, has taught me, "The only way to destroy fear is to destroy the makers of fear, the murderer and the oppressor." A revolutionary is not a criminal nor is she or he an adventurer, and revolutionary violence is nothing more than the most profound means of achieving internal as well as external balance.

I would like to correct and clarify the information given to you by the regime-controlled media and police-state reports associating the Symbionese Liberation Army with the August Seventh.† First of all, statements that August Seventh literature and original communiques were found in the Concord house are completely untrue. The Symbionese Liberation Army is not the August Seventh. In fact, the August Seventh is a counter-revolutionary Oakland city and California state pig plot to discredit revolutionaries and confuse the people. Freedom fighters act only in the interest of the people, they do not unnecessarily shoot down helicopters whose crashing would endanger lives of people in their communities, nor do they credit themselves with events or accidents that occur in which they had no part, nor do they issue threats which they are unprepared to carry out, nor

† The little-known August Seventh Guerrilla Movement was active in 1972–73; they claimed to have shot down an Oakland Police helicopter (the police said the helicopter crashed due to mechanical failure) and murdered a prison guard, among other alleged crimes.

do they expose the nature and whereabouts of their forces, as for example in the recent statement issued by August Seventh saying that armed guerrilla units existed inside the prisons. The events and communiques associated with the August Seventh served only enemy purposes: that is, a statewide lockdown went into effect in the prisons and the people began to think of revolutionary action as that which would endanger their lives and homes. As a member of the SLA, I can tell you that the SLA takes full credit and responsibility for its actions. We acknowledge everything that we do, and if we had shot down a helicopter, we would say so. If I had participated as a decoy in a taxicab incident, I would say so. However, let me tell you not to rely solely on my analysis that the August Seventh and the Oakland and California state political police are one and the same, but instead, just take a look for yourselves, and ask yourselves, whose interest their actions and threats have served, and remind yourselves of the extent to which the police will go to discredit revolutionaries by labeling all street violence as revolutionary activity and by issuing nothing but threatening communiques and then saying that such threats were coming from revolutionaries. It isn't just coincidence that the week the August Seventh issued an idle threat against the life of prison official Procunier was the same week that the California legislature reinstated the death penalty.

About that house in Concord, California. It was a Symbionese Liberation Army information/intelligence headquarters and nothing more. The house was set on fire by me only to melt away any fingerprints that may have been overlooked. It never was intended that the fire would totally destroy the premises, because there was nothing left there that was of any real consequence to us, nor was there any material left behind that could stagnate the functioning ability of the SLA to carry on the struggle. The reports that mass armaments were found in that house is a lie. It is an attempt to frame my two comrade brothers and it is an assertion to cover up the fact that there were no weapons found there. All that remained were three broken BB guns, a couple of malfunctioning gas masks, a few research books, and several liberation posters on the walls. Also, let me tell you that no one living or coming to the house was part of the SLA combat forces. This can be easily verified because, first of all, everyone in SLA combat forces is offensively armed with cyanide bullets in all weapons that they carry, and up until today this had not been the case for SLA information/intelligence units or any SLA support units. At that time, all units but combat units were only defensively armed with handguns that carried no cyanide bullets. Secondly, we can easily verify that the ballistics on the .380 now in the hands of pig agents do not match those of the weapon used in the attack on the Oakland Board of Education. Information/intelligence units or any support units were never allowed to possess or have any contact with combat unit weapons. Beginning January eleventh, however, a directive was issued by the SLA and the Court of the People stating that as of that date, all units of the Symbionese Liberation Army are to be heavily and offensively armed with cyanide bullets in all their weapons at all times. I would like to convey the word, to my two captured compañeros, you have not been forgotten, and you will be defended because there has been no setback and all combat forces are intact.

There really are no words available to me to express what I feel about the capture of my two compañeros. They are in a concentration camp now because none of us were offensively armed, and because I was not aware that they were under attack. But my beautiful brothers, as we have said many times, we learn from our mistakes, and we learn from our active participation in struggle, not from political rhetoric, so we won't cry, but simply fight over, and *right on* with that. A comrade of mine, Bo, says something that I'd like to leave you with: "There are two things to remember about revolution. We are going to get our asses kicked, and we are going to win."

the voice of Donald DeFreeze (Cinque)
Death to the fascist insect that preys upon the life of the people.

January 25, 1974

The police search the abandoned apartment of William and Emily Harris, where they find another "target" list.

February 4, 1974

Patricia Hearst is kidnapped by the SLA – specifically Donald DeFreeze, William Harris, and Angela Atwood – from her apartment at 2603 Benvenue Avenue in Berkeley. Shots are fired (no one is hit). Hearst's fiancé, Steven Weed, is assaulted but manages to escape; their next-door neighbor, UC Berkeley student Steve Suenaga, is also assaulted. Recovering from their minor injuries, both Weed and Suenaga identify the male kidnappers as African American, which later leads authorities to believe that Harris (a former actor) was wearing blackface makeup.

Hearst is imprisoned in a closet in the SLA safehouse at 37 Northridge Avenue in the San Francisco suburb of Daly City. Holding her hostage are five white women (Angela Atwood, Camilla Hall, Emily Harris, Nancy Ling Perry, and Patricia Mizmoon Soltysik), two white men (William Harris and William Wolfe), and one black man (Donald DeFreeze) – the Symbionese Liberation Army.

THE ARREST OF PATRICIA CAMPBELL HEARST
FEBRUARY 4, 1974

SYMBIONESE LIBERATION ARMY
Western Regional Adult Unit

Communique No. 3
February 4, 1974
Subject: Prisoners of War
Target: Patricia Campbell Hearst
daughter of Randolph A. Hearst corporate enemy of the people
Warrant Order: Arrest and protective custody; and if resistance execution
Warrant Issued By: The Court of the People

On the afore stated date, combat elements of the United Federated Forces of the Symbionese Liberation Army armed with cyanide loaded weapons served an arrest warrant upon Patricia Campbell Hearst.

It is the order of this court that the subject be arrested by combat units and removed to a protective area of safety and only upon completion of this condition to notify Unit #4 to give communication of this action.

It is the directive of this court that during this action ONLY, no civilian elements be harmed if possible, and that warning shots be given. However, if any citizens attempt to aid the authorities or interfere with the implementation of this order, they shall be executed immediately.

This court hereby notifies the public and directs all combat units in the future to shoot to kill any civilian who attempts to witness or interfere with any operation conducted by the people's forces against the fascist state.

Should any attempt be made by the authorities to rescue the prisoner, or to arrest or harm any S.L.A. elements, the prisoner is to be executed.

The prisoner is to be maintained in adequate physical and mental condition, and unharmed as long as these conditions are adhered to. Protective custody shall be composed of combat and medical units, to safeguard both the prisoner and her health.

All communications from this court MUST be published in full, in all newspapers, and all other forms of the media. Failure to do so will endanger the safety of the prisoner.

Further communications will follow.

S.L.A.

DEATH TO THE FASCIST INSECT
THAT PREYS UPON THE LIFE OF THE PEOPLE

February 8, 1974

Emily Harris's father, Frederick Schwartz, contacts the FBI to tell them he thinks his daughter and son-in-law are involved in the Hearst kidnapping.

MY NAME IS CINQUE
FEBRUARY 12, 1974

[transcript of audio tape]

the voice of Donald DeFreeze (Cinque)

To those who would bear the hopes and future of our people, let the voice of their guns express the words of freedom. Greetings to the people and fellow comrade brothers and sisters.

My name is Cinque, and to my comrades I am known as Cin. I am a black man and a representative of black people. I hold the rank of General Field Marshal in the United Federated Forces of the Symbionese Liberation Army.

Today I have received an order from the Symbionese War Council, the Court of the People, to the effect that I am ordered to convey the following message in behalf of the SLA, and to insert a taped word of comfort and verification, that Patricia Campbell Hearst is alive and safe.

The Symbionese Liberation Army is the federated union of military-political elements of many different liberation struggles, and of many different races. Our unified purpose is to liberate the oppressed peoples of this nation and to aid other oppressed people around the world in their struggle against fascist imperialism and the robbery of their freedom and homeland. Since this is the purpose and goal of the SLA, it is therefore clear to us, as it will be to all oppressed people, that our interest is to serve and defend the people and not ourselves, since the people shall always come first in our hearts and souls.

The SLA has arrested the subject for the crimes that her mother and father have, by their actions, committed against we, the American people, and the oppressed people of the world. In understanding this charge, we must first understand who the Hearsts are, and who they serve and represent.

Randolph A. Hearst is the corporate chairman of the fascist media empire of the ultra-right Hearst Corporation, which is one of the largest propaganda institutions of this oppressive military dictatorship of the militarily armed corporate state that we now live under in this nation.

The primary goal of this empire is to save and form a necessary propaganda and smokescreen to shield the American people from seeing the realities of the corporate dictatorship that Richard Nixon and Gerald Ford represent. This network of propaganda programs and confusion has succeeded in hiding the truth from the people; that truth being that this nation has suffered its first military-corporate coup and that the Constitution, which some of us still believe in, has been overthrown.

The fascist Hearst Corporation, composed of, firstly, a national newspaper syndicate, which includes the San Francisco *Examiner* and *Chronicle,* and others which jump from California and to as far away as New York and Philadelphia.

Secondly, a magazine monopoly composed of over thirteen publications, which include, for example, *House Beautiful, Harper's Bazaar, Town and Country,* and *Cosmopolitan.*

Thirdly, a TV and radio station empire across the nation,

with production of propaganda fields of both national and international use.

Fourth, ownership of vast areas of real estate in the United States and Mexico: forest, grasslands, and cattle farms.

All of this is directly connected to Washington and the corporate dictatorship of Richard Nixon and Gerald Ford. That is to say that the Hearst empire is one of the empires of the ruling class and whose interests is the rich and are in direct contradiction with the interests of the people. Therefore, they are enemies of the people.

Mrs. Randolph A. Hearst is a member of the University of California Board of Regents and is responsible, along with others appointed by Governor Ronald Reagan, for the lowering of funds and the investments of our California tax moneys in corporations, which have interests and do gain profit from the robbery, oppression, and genocide carried out by fascist and racist governments around the world and within the United States itself.

The Regents, with the support of Mrs. Hearst, have time and time again been requested by we, the people, to not invest our money in such fascist corporations as General Motors, Westinghouse, Gulf, Standard Oil, Bank of America, and others, who have and do serve and gain profit from the oppression, robbery, and murder that is committed against black people of South Africa, where seventy thousand black children a year die from malnutrition; against white people of Ireland, where U.S.-trained British soldiers shoot down in the street Irish fathers and mothers, as U.S.-manufactured tear gas suffogates, suffocates Irish children as their older sisters and brothers rot in British concentration camps; against the freedom of the Philippine people where United States and Marcos puppet soldiers use U.S.-manufactured napalm to attempt to burn away the spirit of freedom from the hearts and souls of the poor and starving.

The UC Board of Regents, one of California's largest foreign investors, supports, through its investments, the murder of thousands of black men, women, and children of Mozambique, Angola, and Rhodesia, murder designed to destroy the spirit that all humanity longs for.

With all these crimes placed bepore, before the Board of Regents and Mrs. Hearst, with all the pleas from the people to stop supporting these corporations and the murder of thousands of men, women, and children, the Board and Mrs. Hearst did not raise one voice in protest, or refuse to be a party to these crimes committed against these people, and those committed against the American people.

For these acts and others, the Court of the People hold the Hearst family accountable for their crimes and hold that they are enemies of the people.

We of the Symbionese Liberation Army hold that the Hearst Corporation and the Hearst family and the Board of Regents, as well as the corporate state which they support and aid, are enemies of the people, and as such that the people have the legal and human right and duty to attack said enemy according to the forms of war taken by the oppressed people against any enemy or murderer and oppressor to regain their freedom and liberty and we give love to their children and people.

It is therefore the directive of this court that before any form of negotiation for the release of the subject prisoner be initiated, that an action of good faith be shown on the part of the Hearst family to allow the court and the oppressed people of this world and this nation to ascertain as to the real interests and cooperative attitude of the Hearst family and, in so doing, show some form of repentance for the murder and suffering they have aided and profited from, and this good-faith gesture is to be in the form of a token gesture to the oppressed people that they aid the corporate state in robbing and removing their rights to freedom and liberty.

This gesture is to be in the form of food to the needy and the unemployed, and to which the following instructions are directed to be followed to the letter.

In closing, and speaking personally for myself, and as a father of two children, I wish to say to Mr. Hearst and Mrs. Hearst that I, as well as the forces under my command for the authority of the Court of the People, are not savage killers and madmen, and we do hold a high moral value to life. We value a life very deeply, and with all the spirit that we as human beings can bring forth in our hearts. But speaking as a father, I am quite willing to lose both my children, if by that action I could save thousands of white, black, yellow, and red children from a life of suffering, exploitation, and murder, and I am therefore quite willing to carry out the execution of your daughter to save the life of starving men, women, and children of every race, and I am also, along with the loyal men and women of many races who love the people, quite willing to give our lives to free the people at any cost.

And if as you and others might so naively believe that we will lose, let it be known that even in death we will win, for the very ashes of this fascist nation will mark our very graves.

the voice of Patricia Hearst

Mom, Dad, I'm okay. I had a few scrapes and stuff, but, um, they washed them up and they're getting okay and I caught a cold, but they're giving me pills for it and stuff. I'm not being starved or beaten or unnecessarily frightened. Um, I've heard some press reports, and so I know that Steve and all the neighbors are okay and that no one was really hurt. And I also know that the SLA members here are very upset about press distortions of what's been happening. They have nothing to do with the August Seventh Movement. That they have not been shooting down helicopters or shooting down innocent people in the streets.

I'm kept blindfolded usually so that I can't identify anyone. Um, my hands are, are often tied, but generally, um, they're not. And, um, um, I'm not gagged or anything, and I'm comfortable, and I think you can tell that I'm not really terrified or anything and I am okay.

I was very upset though to hear about, um, police rushing in on that house in Oakland, and I was really glad that I wasn't there. And I would appreciate it if, um, everyone would just calm down and not try to find me and not be making identifications because they're not only endangering me but they're endangering themselves.

I'm with a combat unit that's armed with automatic weapons and there's also a medical team here and, um, there's no way that I will be released until they let me go, so it won't do any good for somebody to come in here and try to get me out by force. These people aren't just a bunch of nuts. They've been really honest with me but, um, they're perfectly willing to die for what they're doing, and I want to get out of here but the only way I'm going to is if we do it their way, and I just hope that you'll do what they say, Dad, and just do it quickly.

Um, I've been stopping and starting this tape myself, so that I can collect my thoughts. That's why there are so many stops in it. I'm not being forced to say any of this. Um, I think it's really important that you take their requests very seriously about, um, not arresting any other SLA members and, and about following their good-faith request to the letter. Um, I just want to get out of here and see everyone again and, and be back with Steve.

The SLA is, is very interested in seeing how, how you're taking this, Dad, and they want to make sure that you are, are really serious and listening to what they're saying, um, and they think that you've been taking this whole thing a lot more seriously than the police and the, the FBI and other federal people have been taking it. And, uh, it seems to be getting to the point where they're not worried about you so much as they're worrying about other people, or at least I am. It's, um, it's really up to you to make sure that these people don't, don't jeopardize my life by charging in and doing stupid things, and I hope that you'll make sure that they don't do anything else like, like that Oakland house business.

These, um, the SLA people really have been honest with me and, and I really, I mean I feel pretty sure that I'm going to get out of here if everything goes the way they want it to, and I think you should feel that way too and, and try not to worry so much. I mean I know it's hard but [*sighs*] I heard that Mom was really upset and that all [*sighs*], everybody was at home and, and I mean I hope this puts you a little bit at ease so that, and that you know that I, that I really, that I really am all right. Um, I just hope

I can get back to everybody really soon.

The SLA has ideological ties with the IRA, the people's struggle in the Philippines and the socialist people in, um, Puerto Rico in their struggle for independence, and they consider themselves to be soldiers who are fighting and aiding these people.

I am a prisoner of war and so are the two men in San Quentin. I'm being treated in accordance with the Geneva Convention, one of the conditions being that I am not being tried for crimes which I'm not responsible for.

I'm here because I am a member of a ruling class family, and I think you can begin to see the analogy. The people in San Quen, the two men in San Quentin, are being held and, and are going to be tried simply because they are members of the SLA and not because they've done anything. Witnesses to the shooting of Foster saw black men and, um, and two white men have been arrested for this.

You're being told this so that, um, you'll understand why I was kidnapped, um, and so that you'll understand that whatever happens to the two prisoners is going to happen to me. You have to understand that I am held to be innocent the same way the two men in San Quentin are innocent, that they are simply members of the group, and had not done anything themselves to warrant their arrest. They apparently were part of an intelligence unit and have never executed anyone themselves.

The SLA has declared war against the government and it's important that you understand that this, that they know what they're doing and they understand what their actions mean, and that you realize that this is not considered by them to be just a simple kidnapping, and that you don't treat it that way and say, "Oh, I don't know why she was taken." I'm telling you now why this happened so that you'll know and so that you'll have something to use, some knowledge to try to get me out of here. If you can get the food thing organized before the nineteenth, then that's okay, and it would just speed up my release.

Um, today is Friday the eighth and in Kuwait the commandos negotiated the release of their hostages and they left the country. Bye.

the voice of Donald DeFreeze (Cinque)

Um, Mr. Hearst, um, as your daughter said, uh, she is being held under the international codes of war regarding prisoners of war, and as she is not going to be, uh, harmed in any manner unless any attempt is made to release her by force. She is being properly treated, properly fed, and she has an exercise area, um, fresh air and so forth, uh, and she is not being harmed in any fashion. Uh, and this is also related to our captured soldiers that are being held in San Quentin, and we hope that they will receive the same treatment according to the international codes of war.

Um, we understand from the, uh, national reports and so forth that the, um, police authorities and others are attempting, um, to place the responsibility upon us, in saving the life of your daughter and to distort and mislead the realities of the facts of the matter. However, we wish to express to you, and to the authorities, and to the public, that, uh, whatever happens to your daughter will be totally your responsibility, and the responsibility of the authorities which you represent. Her life will be maintained in the fashion that is according to the terms of war, and if they, and yourself, violate these, her life and the blood of that will be upon your hands only.

In regards to communications, um, for, uh, security reasons, and that because of where we are at, that, that is not, uh, possible for us to maintain a continuous flow of communications with you. So don't expect, uh, phone calls, uh, communications three or four times a week, because they won't come.

Uh, when the, uh, stated good-faith gesture is conducted, and we, uh, have means to ascertain as to if they are, we will begin negotiations for the release of your daughter. Until then, you can be sure, and, uh, have our word, uh, whatever that may be to you, that, uh, we will carry out, uh, our word to the letter, and we mean exactly what we say.

Death to the fascist insect that preys upon the life of the people.

A SYMBOLIC GESTURE OF GOOD FAITH

FEBRUARY 12, 1974

A.

We have heard it said that Mr. Hearst wants to save his daughter, we want to save all the children and people. In an effort to answer some of the basic needs of the people, we are asking for a symbolic gesture of good faith from this representative of the corporate state. Each person with one of the following cards is to be given $70.00 worth of meats, vegetables, and dairy products: all people with welfare cards, social security pension cards, food stamp cards, disabled veteran cards, medical cards, parole or probation papers, and jail or bail release slips. So that all those with such cards have time, and will not be forced to stand waiting in long lines, the time for the distribution of this food must extend over a four week period, beginning February 19th. On each Tuesday, Thursday, and Saturday for four successive weeks, each person with one of the listed cards can go to publicized stores and pick up their food.

1. The stores where people can go are to be clearly designated and publicized in each of the communities listed below, and they are to be within easy access to the people of those communities. There must be at least 5 stores as distribution points within each community; these distribution points should be major stores within the community, we suggest such stores as Safeway and

Mayfair.

2. The meat, vegetables, and dairy products must be of top quality, and in ample supply during all store hours.

3. TO THE PEOPLE: If you are not receiving your food, all you have to do is voice your discontent in the streets, at bus stops, movie theatres, etc. and we will hear about it. Also anyone facing any interference from the police state in the way of harassment should voice their discontent. The people's army calls upon community groups such as Nirobi College in East Palo Alto, Glide Memorial Church in San Francisco, and The Black Teachers Caucus, the National Welfare Rights Organization, United Farm Workers, AIM, Third World Womens Alliance, United Prisoner's Union, as well as representatives from people's news services such as Getting Together, Kalayan, Triple Jeopardy, Black Panther Party, The Anvil, and others to act as observers and coordinators to see to it that the aged and disabled receive their food and ways to transport it and shop for it, AND to see to it that NO police-state agents, in or out of uniform, are allowed to be in the areas of food distribution, or photograph or harass the people.

4. Stores in each of the following cities or communities are to serve as distribution points:

San Francisco (Mission District, Chinatown, Hunters Point, The Fillmore)
Oakland (East and West)
Richmond
East Palo Alto
Delano
Santa Rosa

Los Angeles (Watts, Compton, East Los Angeles)

B –

1. The document the emblem and meaning of the seven-headed cobra that is in the possession of police state authorities shall be placed in newspapers and other forms of the media in its exact form, not omitting any area.

2. The document that is enclosed regarding the declaration of war and the goals of The S.L.A. shall also be placed in its total form in newspapers and other forms of the media.

3. A copy of all these stated documents, along with a full copy of the tape enclosed recorded by myself and Pat Hearst is to be distributed to the media for publication.

4. The news media is warned that all attempts to mislead the public concerning the intentions of The S.L.A., or to confuse the public by withholding or omitting sections of the tape or S.L.A. documents, jeopardizes the prisoner.

IF THIS GESTURE OF GOOD FAITH IS NOT MET THEN WE WILL ASSUME THAT THERE IS NO BASIS FOR NEGOTIATIONS, AND WE WILL NO LONGER TAKE AND MAINTAIN IN GOOD HEALTH AND SPIRITS PRISONERS OF WAR.

S.L.A.

February 13, 1974

Patricia Hearst's parents, Randolph and Catherine Hearst, appear before reporters in front of their Hillsborough mansion to say that they will do everything they can to guarantee the safe release of their daughter.

THIS IS NOT A RACIAL THING

FEBRUARY 16, 1974

[transcript of audio tape]

the voice of Patricia Hearst

Dad, Mom, I'm making this tape to, uh, let you know that I'm still okay and to explain a few things, I hope.

First, about the good-faith gesture. There was some misunderstanding about that, and, um, you should do what you can and then they understand that, that you want to meet their demands and that, uh, and they, they had every intention that you should be able to, um, meet their demands. They were not trying to present an unreasonable request. It was never intended that you feed the whole state. Um, so whatever you come up with basically is okay and just do it as fast as you can, and everything's, everything will be fine.

Um, but the SLA is really mad about, um, the certain attempts to, uh, make receiving the food be, um, you know, receiving goods that have been gotten by extortion. And, uh, they just, they don't want people to be harassed by the police or by anybody else, and, um, I mean I hope you can do something about that, and if you can't, well, I mean, they'll do something about it. So, you shouldn't worry about that too much.

Um, also, I would like to emphasize that I am alive and that I am well, and that, uh, in spite of what certain tape experts seem to think, I am, I mean I'm fine. And, uh, it's really depressing to hear people talk about me like I'm dead. And, um, you know I just, I can't explain what that's like. What it does, also, is that it, it begins to convince other people that maybe I am dead. And, um, and when everybody is convinced that I am dead, well, then it gives the FBI an excuse to come in here and try to pull me out. And uh, I'm sure that Mr. Bates understands that, uh, if the FBI has to come in and get me out by force, that they won't have time to decide who not to kill. They'll just have to kill everyone. And, um, yeah, I don't particularly want to die that way. Um, so I, I hope you will realize that everything is okay and that, um, you know, just back off for a while, there will be plenty of time for investigating later.

I am basically an example, a symbolic warning, not only to you but, um, to everyone, that, uh, that there are people who are not going to accept, um, to accept your support of, um, of other governments and that, um, basically suppressed and, and murder other people, and, uh, this is a warning to everybody.

And it's also to show what can be done when it's necessary, that people can be fed, and that, and to show that it's too bad that it has to happen this way, to make people see that, that there are people who need food. But, um, you know maybe something can be done about that, so that things like this won't have to happen again.

And they're also, the SLA's also very annoyed about attempts by the press and by authorities to turn this into a racial issue. It's not. This is a political issue and this is a political action that they've taken. And anyone who really reads the stated objectives of the SLA can see very clearly that this is not a racial thing. And, um, I hope there won't be any more confusion about that.

Turn over my notes here, so [*laughter*], um, I am being held as a prisoner of war and not as anything else, I mean I'm being treated in accordance with international codes of war. So, I mean they shouldn't listen or believe what anybody else says about the way I'm being treated. This is the way that I am being treated. I am not left alone and I am not just shoved off, I mean, I am fine, and, uh, I am not being starved, and I am not being beaten or tortured, really.

Um, also, since I am an example, and it's really important that everybody understand that, you know, I am an example and a warning. And because of this, it's very important to the SLA that I return safely. And, um, so people should stop acting like I'm dead, and Mom should get out of her black dress. That doesn't help at all.

And, uh, I mean I, I wish you'd try to understand the position that I'm in. I'm right in the middle, and I have to depend on what all other, all kinds of other people are going to do. And it's really, it's really hard for me to hear, hear about reports of, you know, and, uh, I mean I hope you understand and try to do something.

I know that a lot of people have written and, and they're really concerned about me and my safety, and about what you're going through. And, you know, I want them all to know that I'm okay and, and to understand that I'll be okay as long as the SLA demands are met, and as long as the two prisoners in San Quentin are okay.

And, um, and as long as the FBI doesn't come in here. I mean, that's, that is my biggest worry. Um, because I, because I think I can get out of here alive as long as they don't come busting in.

And I really think you should understand that the SLA does have an interest in my returning. And, um, and try not to worry so much. And just do what you can and, and I mean, I know you're doing everything. Take care of Steve and, I don't know, just hurry. Bye.

On Wednesday, Solzhenitsyn was exiled to West Germany.

the voice of Donald DeFreeze (Cinque)

This is General Field Marshal Cin speaking.

We wish to clarify what your daughter has said about our request for a good-faith gesture on your part.

The people are awaiting your gesture. You may rest assured that we are quite able to assess the extent of your sincerity in this matter and we will accept a sincere effort on your part.

We are quite able and aware of the extent of your capabilities, as we are also aware of the needs of the people.

Death to the fascist insect that preys upon the life of the people.

I'M THE NIGGER THAT HUNTS YOU NOW

FEBRUARY 21, 1974

[transcript of audio tape]

the voice of Donald DeFreeze (Cinque)

To those who would bear the hopes and faith of our people, that the voice of their guns express the words of freedom.

Greetings to the people, comrades, sisters, and brothers. General Field Marshal Cin speaking.

The Symbionese War Council, the Court of the People, has just finished hearing tapes and hearing some of the news reports and statements made by the Hearst family concerning the arrest of Patricia Campbell Hearst. In the court's second tape by Patricia, it was said that any good-faith gesture on the part of the Hearst empire would be "basically okay."

We, however, understand that Patricia wants to come home as soon as possible, and that this statement was clearly misinterpreted as meaning that an untrue gesture of good faith and regret would be accepted by the people. And this is not the case. Therefore, at the end of that tape stated by Patricia, I myself, by the direction of the court, stated the feeling of the court and thereby clarify the request of the people.

That statement reads as follows:

"We wish to clarify what your daughter has said about our

request for a good-faith gesture on your part. The people are awaiting your gesture. You may rest assured that we are quite able to assess the extent of your sincerity in this matter, and will accept a sincere effort on your part. We are quite able and aware of the extent of your capabilities, as we are also aware of the needs of the people."

The Hearst empire has attempted to mislead the people and to deceive them by claiming to put forth a good-faith gesture of two million dollars. This amount is not at all a good-faith gesture, but rather is an act of throwing a few crumbs to the people, forcing them to fight over it amongst themselves.

We have had a court hearing concerning both the actions of the enemy Hearst family and the Hearst empire as a whole, and the media, and the combined responsible gesture of good faith.

We have chosen first to expose a sampling of the extent of the Hearst empire, which includes the Hearst Foundation, the Hearst Corporation empire, and Mr. and Mrs. Hearst's personal assets. The assets of the Hearsts' wealth include the following:

A silver mine and thousands of acres of land in Mexico, land acreage in Hawaii, and seventy thousand acres of timberland in Northern California valued at millions of dollars. A cattle ranch near San Luis Obispo, orange groves in Florida, a duck club and rice paddies outside of Marysville, California. Small land holdings and homes in Hillsborough, New York, and San Diego. Each valued at well over one-half million dollars.

2. Personal stocks. Large interests in IBM, Beatrice Foods, Exxon, the Sugar Bowl Corporation, and Safeway Stores, United Airlines, and Hughes Airways. And huge holdings in drug companies, ore industries, paper companies, lumber companies, and

cattle ranches.

3. Miscellaneous personal items. A collection of antique paintings, Chinese screens, and Greek vases. Twenty-four vases each valued at ten thousand dollars each. A collection of Oriental rugs given to him by his personal friend, the Shah of Iran. The family has also received numerous gifts over the years from other longtime personal friends such as Howard Hughes.

The Hearst Foundation. The Hearst Foundation is a front for the Hearst fortune. The foundation serves as a tax loophole for that fortune. The foundation donates an estimated three million dollars yearly to established charities to maintain its status as a foundation. The one-and-one-half million dollars proposed to be coming from the foundation is nothing more than half of what that foundation is legally required to donate annually in order to maintain its foundation status.

The assets of the Hearst Corporation have been stated many times. However, I will restate them again as some specific factors. As we all know, the Hearst Corporation is composed of a chain of magazines and newspapers. However, I wish to point out two specific ones as examples. *Cosmopolitan* magazine reaps profits of seven to eight million dollars per year. Another is *House Beautiful,* which reaps profits of three to four million dollars a year. The Hearst Corporation is also composed of, as mentioned before, a chain of TV stations and feature-film industries, also ownership of lumber companies and partnership in large stockholdings in General Motors, as well as land holdings in each of the cities where the newspaper chains operate: for example, ownership of one square block in New York City, with the land alone valued in hundreds of millions of dollars, as well as land

and buildings in England, Australia, and Europe.

In total, the Hearst empire along with Mr. and Mrs. Hearst's personal wealth does in fact run into the hundreds and hundreds of millions. Even if Mr. Hearst was to give all that to the people, with personal friends such as the Shah of Iran and Howard Hughes, he would suffer no losses. However, even if Mr. Hearst were to give all of that to the people, he could never pay the people back for the past losses of their children and freedom, nor for the current suffering they are now under.

We also wish to point out that when necessary the enemy cannot adjust its losses to correspond to its interest at any given time.

It is in the direct interest of Mr. Hearst to comply with the demand for food, not because he finds it necessary to feed the people, but rather because he must secure and protect one of his possessions: his daughter Patricia. Thus, he finds a way to change the proposal in acceptable laws which allow him to distribute charitable rather than ransom goods.

In the same vein, when the state and enemy corporations wish to aid such countries as South Africa, the Philippines, South Vietnam, or Ireland in securing brutal dictatorships which rob and murder the people, no existing laws are honored and no one responsible goes to prison for the rest of their lives. This is typified in the Watergate scheme and the U.S. deliberate violation of the United Nations-sanctioned international embargo of Rhodesian goods.

On the other hand, any time the interests of the people are at hand there is an enemy law to counteract those interests, and of course the people are forced to abide by them. In understanding this, we come to understand why the U.S. has more prisons, and the largest numbers of laws to control the people, that has ever been recorded in the history of humans on this earth. These laws are created to imprison the people, and by that protect the rich from the poor.

The plan proposed by Mr. Hearst is not at all acceptable as a gesture of good faith in its present form. It shall be acceptable only insofar as it totally meets the specifications as listed in the following:

1. That an additional four million dollars be added to the two million dollars already allotted, making a total of six million dollars to be used for the purchase of food. We recognize that at wholesale prices available to Mr. Hearst in his designated "Peoples In Need" charity organization, he will be able to feed all who come to receive food. We specify wholesale prices here because we did not intend for Safeway or any other supermarket to make a profit from feeding the poor, nor do we intend for this to be another program which subsidizes the food industry.

2. That this total six-million-dollar figure be disbursed to the cities of San Francisco, Oakland, and East Palo Alto. That an adequate number of distribution centers be made available to various communities in these cities: San Francisco – Mission District, Chinatown, Hunters Point, the Western Addition; Oakland – East and West; Palo Alto – East Palo Alto.

3. That all foods distributed be of top quality, and that all canned goods and dry foods be matched with their equal amounts of top-quality fresh meats, dairy products, and produce, and that no attempt be made to distribute garbage, or clothes, or surplus storage foods or government commodities to

the people.

4. That seventy dollars be given over a one-month period to each family coming to receive food. That is, by the end of one month's time, a total of seventy dollars of food will have been given to each family. This is to be done during the first month of operation of the program. If this means problems with food storage at the distribution center, then it will be a necessity to have an expansion of the number of centers, as well as the number of days and hours that the centers are open.

It has always been the intention of the SLA and the Court of the People that a substantial number of families in at least several communities be able to receive their amount of food during this one-month period that would meet some of their needs, and in addition assure that the people get something more than another extended program which could be abandoned by the Hearsts at any time without the people having ever really received anything. For we have no basis on which to formulate a trust that an enemy of the people could surely extend a gesture for one year or for any ongoing process. Further. it is the decision of this court that six dollars per month for a year is in no way beneficial as seventy dollars for one month.

5. No names shall be taken or any other form of identification or any addresses from any peoples who come to receive food. Any people who come to receive food shall get it. There shall be absolutely no questionnaires, form, or any other type of program processing, which peoples coming to get food should have to go through. And that no form of identification or verification of need other than a simple verbal request for food shall be required.

6. That members of the coalition of the people's community organizations and groups be made up of not only the six example organizations named, but any people's organizations who wish to participate with San Francisco's Western Addition Project Area Committee, known as WAPAC, acting as chairman if they so desire. And that this coalition act solely in the capacity of observers and coordinators, and not negotiators between the SLA combat forces and Mr. Hearst, to see to it that the aged and disabled receive their food, and ways to transport it and shop for it. And to see to it that no police agents in or out of uniform are allowed to be in the areas of food distribution, or photograph or harass the people. And that is to be the leadership of the coalition who should see to it that the distribution centers are run in the true spirit of revolutionary cooperatives, with no bureaucratic overseers or hirelings in the people's distribution centers.

7. That we hereby request that the San Francisco Western Addition Project Area Committee, known as WAPAC, is hereby designated, if they accept this request, as chairman of the coalition, and has full veto power in the actions and activities of the coalition. We request this and ask this because that organization's example of showing the people that they serve only the interest of the people, and that they desire to feed the people by any means necessary, and that they did not compromise the needs of the people for the sake of their leadership positions or for the sake of their organization – rather, without being requested, stepped forward to show themselves to be in interest of the people.

8. That this tape and a transcript of it be published and

printed in full, omitting nothing, in all forms of the media.

9. That the total amount of six million dollars be allotted to your designated "Peoples in Need" or charity organizations within twenty-four hours of receipt of this order and that the food be available to the people within one week of receipt of this order. Should this order be rejected, all further communications shall be suspended and the prisoner will be maintained according to the terms of the international codes of war concerning prisoners of war and will be maintained in that status until such time as the status of our captive soldiers is changed. Should any attempt be made to rescue the subject prisoner or to injure or capture our captive soldiers, the subject is to be executed immediately.

10. Once we see compliance with these specifications and the program well underway, then, as we have previously stated, we will begin negotiations for the release of your daughter. The Court of the People also wishes to state that we understand the position of different political organizations requested by the court to oversee the distribution of food. We understand that refusal to participate is partially due to the inherent dangers placed upon the leadership or the organization as a whole when affiliated with the SLA is stated. We also feel that it is partially due to a lack of understanding of the common enemy, as well as a desire to accept reform and revisionism, which are pacifiers against true change in revolution. But for those who do see the necessity to participate in this action and who do recognize the needs of the people, we again state that we are asking only that you function as coordinators and observers for distribution of food, and that you are not to serve as liaisons, spokesmans, or

negotiators for the SLA unless clearly defined as such by writing or by tape.

In our previous communiques, we called upon all community groups, including certain specific ones, to act as observers and coordinators. There are basically three stances these groups can show to the people:

1. Some stand with the people and actively accept the responsibility of working and fighting for the people.

2. Others don't stand at all.

3. Some stand and then slide up next to the enemy's power, serve with the individual organization instead of the people.

Through this we grew to understand that where an organization or a group of organizations is presented to the enemy as in this case, the enemy will attempt to only negotiate with the political leadership that is most willing to compromise the need and interest of the people and who have the most willingness to call for reform rather than freedom for all people. This is not to condemn these organizations or their leadership but rather to suggest that the people work with these groups and organizations, and educate them and their leaders to serve the interest of the people at all cost and at all times.

We also wish to express to the people how important it is to recognize the meaning of the enemy strategy. We must recognize that enemy propaganda and psychological warfare will be used throughout the struggle for freedom. We must combat enemy attempts to demoralize us, for in the face of the failure to achieve military solutions against the people's army, the enemy has to then step up its efforts in the propaganda war.

Their aim is to, one, to prevent a liberation movement from

getting underway by destroying it at its source, that is by undermining the will to fight. And, two, where revolutionary warfare has actually begun, to conquer it by political means. That is to say by granting just sufficient political, economic, and social reform for the moment to encourage all but the so-called extremists to abandon the struggle and then kill off the leadership of the people, as in the period of King and Malcolm, and then reinstate as a deity oppression and murder of the then-defenseless people.

In stating these facts we wish to say that the collective leadership of the SLA would not under any circumstances or any terms compromise our position or that of the people's freedom. And no one should attempt to speak for us or assume that they, by word or action, can compromise any request made in behalf of the people of the SLA.

On this point we wish to state that the organizations who wish to take part in feeding the people should also cry out for the thousands of children of all colors who have been murdered and starved by the enemy state. They should cry out for the millions of children of all races who are starving and dying now, and not just cry out for the safety of only one human being, who just happens to be the daughter of the enemy of the people. Fight and cry out in defense of millions and save the children. And by this action you will save also the life of one who has never seen the robbed, or knew that the riches of her life were the spoils of a robber and murderer.

It is in the judgment of this court that the Hearst family and the Hearst Corporation seems to be more foolishly concerned with the identities of supposed SLA elements rather than with the admission to the people of the crimes committed against the people by the Hearst empire. An act of good faith, in a choice shown to the people, not to the SLA, the Hearst empire should demonstrate a change of interest, regret for his crimes against the people, and a firm decision that they will no longer be a party to such actions in the future.

They should also demonstrate that they are not only concerned with freeing and making a better life for Patricia, but also freeing and making a better life for all the people.

However, they have seemingly said by their actions that they know me, and therefore they do not have to repent for their crimes.

However, to this I would say yes. You do, indeed, know me. You have always known me. I'm that nigger you have hunted and feared night and day. I'm that nigger you have killed hundreds of my peoples in a vain hope of finding. I'm that nigger that is no longer just the hunted, robbed, and murdered. I'm the nigger that hunts you now.

Yes, you know me. You know us all. You know me, I'm the wetback. You know me, I'm the gook, the broad, the servant, the spic.

Yes indeed, you know us all, and we know you: the oppressor, murderer, and robber. And you have hunted and robbed and exploited us all. Now we are the hunters that will give you no rest. And we'll not compromise the freedom of our children.

Death to the fascist insect that preys upon the life of the people.

the voice of Patricia Hearst

Today is the nineteenth and yesterday the Shah of Iran had two people executed at dawn.

February 22, 1974

Ludlow Kramer is named the head of People in Need (PIN) by Randolph Hearst. The first of five food giveaways demanded by the SLA occurs in San Francisco, Richmond, East Palo Alto, and Oakland. Insanity reigns: food is thrown from the backs of trucks at clamoring mobs fighting and screaming; many people are injured, with one woman losing her eye.

Randolph Hearst later issues a counterproposal to the SLA: he will place an additional four million dollars into an escrow account for food distribution, but only when his daughter is released unharmed.

March 3, 1974

The Hearsts hold a press conference and request that the SLA let them speak with their daughter directly.

A WARNING TO THE FASCIST MILITARY STATE

MARCH 9, 1974

[transcript of audio tape]

the voice of Angela Atwood (Gelina)

To those who would bear the hopes and future of our people, let the voice of their guns express the words of freedom.

Greetings to the people and comrade sisters and brothers. My name is Gelina and I am a general in the Symbionese Liberation Army.

I am speaking to you on behalf of the Symbionese War Council, the Court of the People, and on behalf of the Symbionese Federation as a whole.

I speak the deepest expression of freedom and cry out for revolutionary unity. With profound love we greet the Black Liberation Army, the Weather Underground, the BGF and WO, and those brave women and men who by force of arms have shown that there is no compromise for freedom, and that the meaning of the Federation's codes of unity holds true: That to die a race and be born a nation is to become free.

There have been many on the Left who, without a clear understanding, have condemned the actions of the SLA and the people's forces who have chosen to fight rather than talk. These speakers condemn without clearly recognizing that our actions are a direct response to the vicious and murderous actions of the enemy corporate state against the people.

It has been claimed that we are destroying the Left, but in truth an unarmed and non-fighting Left is doomed, as the people of Chile can sadly testify.

The analysis of these so-called leaders who presume to speak for the people can be traced to one of two qualities: Either they are cowards afraid of revolutionary violence because it is a direct threat to their personal security and comfort, or they are opportunists who have personal gains in allowing the enemy to enslave or oppress and tranquilize the people.

The dream, and indeed it is a dream, of this reactionary leadership is that the enemy corporate state will willingly give the stolen riches of the earth back to the people and that this will be accomplished through compromising talk and empty words.

In reality, the enemy state forces the people to buy back the goods that the people themselves have produced at the price of blood. To this, our bullets scream loudly. The enemy's bloodthirsty greed will be destroyed by the growing spirit of the people and their thirst for freedom.

The actions of the SLA are based on a clear understanding and analysis of the enemy and its actions against the lives and freedom of the people. We call upon the people to judge for themselves whether our tactics of waging struggle are correct or incorrect in fighting the enemy by any means necessary.

The SLA and the Court of the People wish to state to the people the reasons behind the present suspension of communications and negotiations.

The people have been experiencing the true meaning of the

Hearst empire's sincerity – that true meaning being deception and lies. Throughout the previous period of communication between the SLA and the Hearst empire, the SLA and the Court of the People have dealt truthfully with all concerned. We have at all times followed our revolutionary principles of utilizing our three weapons of war: our guns, our determination, and the truth. And this means that we will never say anything that we do not totally mean to do.

We wish to place before the people a comparison of the sincere actions of the SLA and the counteractions of the Hearst empire.

1. The Court of the People requested that all documents of the court be printed in full, omitting nothing. The Hearst empire omitted Communiques One and Two concerning the Foster operations and court documents that were to be published. Also the meaning of the seven-headed cobra on the reverse side of the document showing the emblem of the SLA was purposely omitted.

2. The Court of the People requested that seventy dollars' worth of top-quality food, including an equal balance of drystuffs and canned goods and fresh meat, poultry, produce, and dairy products, be given to poor families in various Bay Area communities as a gesture of good faith so that negotiations for Patricia Hearst might begin. But Hearst and the Hearst empire contributed two million dollars to People in Need, a program set up by Hearst in reaction to the request of the SLA. Instead of issuing a type and quality of food stipulated, PIN showed contempt for the people through disorganization in distribution of surplus commodities instead of top-quality fresh meats,

vegetables, and produce. PIN also intended to sham the people by trying to distribute hog feed instead of top-quality drystuffs. The people had to stand in long lines for hours only to be treated as dogs when the PIN food was thrown at them. Many people were injured by police in East Oakland.

3. The SLA showed severe displeasure with the meager Hearst contribution and with the Hearst PIN program. The SLA reissued its guidelines for an adequate and equitable food distribution and requested that the Hearst empire add an additional four million dollars to the measly two million dollars. In a communique the SLA proved the Hearst trickery by stating just how rich and powerful the Hearsts and the Hearst empire really are. Randolph Hearst responded deceitfully that he could not meet financially the SLA requests, and stated in typical capitalist fashion that the situation was out of his hands. As if Hearst had no connection with the Hearst Corporation, the corporation, supposedly out of the kindness of its corporate heart, responded that it would provide the additional four million dollars, but only after Patricia Hearst is released.

Hearst and the Hearst Corporation assumed that the SLA and the people were inexperienced in the area of corporate trickery, and so they said that they would give two million dollars upon Patricia Hearst's release and the rest in January 1975. However, the people have experienced such trickery too many times in the past to ever be fooled by it again. SLA elements were at Wounded Knee and we too honored the elders' decision to cease the occupation. But we will not forget the lesson that we learned from our brothers and sisters there: One thing above all, never trust the words of the enemy.

Hearst's PIN program stated that it would follow the SLA distribution guidelines. However, instead of seventy dollars' worth of top-quality food, the people have gotten eight dollars' worth of mediocre food. Instead of fresh meat, half the people received one chicken. Many stood in long, cold lines for only a bag full of cabbages, while others stood in line and got nothing at all.

PIN said it distributed thirty thousand bags of food. But this lie was revealed by WAPAC and the Coalition, which said only fifteen thousand walked away with food. After the second day of food distribution, WAPAC and the Coalition issued their reports on Hearst's PIN program.

The SLA and the Court of the People and the People themselves want to see this report printed in full in all forms of the media. There has never been any uncensored, uncut media reporting of any statement made by the Coalition speakers. Ludlow Kramer has boasted the well-known lies that Hearst's program has carried out the terms of the SLA-prescribed good-faith gesture. The people know his words don't make no bag of cabbages into meat.

The Court of the People have a clear understanding of the actions of the Hearsts and the Hearst empire as a whole, in regards to its deceit and silence concerning its interests and crimes against the people.

It is no surprise that Mrs. Hearst has never once said anything about her activities on the University of California Board of Regents and its policy of financing corporations who operate internationally and exploit the hungry and oppressed peoples of the earth.

It is no coincidence that Mr. Hearst has remained silent about his vast interest in the Safeway Stores, Inc., and Exxon, because it is very important that the people of this country not ask questions about these interests.

It is very important to the enemy that people do not begin to question why it is that the same man who is so concerned for bilingual education for Chicano people is also the same man who owns vast stock interests in Safeway Stores, Inc., and thousands of acres of land robbed from Chicano people in California. And a silver mine and thousands of acres of land in Mexico that the Hearst empire has exploited from the peoples in Mexico.

Mr. and Mrs. Hearst, by constantly maintaining the secure position where they are not forced to reveal their interests and crimes, and without really conceding anything to the people, hope to gain the release of the prisoner.

In our analysis of enemy strategy we find multiple reasons for why the Hearst empire has not complied with our request.

First, by frustrating the people, forcing them to continually return to food distribution centers, stand in long lines and receive eight dollars' worth of food, the Hearst empire attempted to discredit the political point of the action.

Secondly, by handing out surplus and low-grade donated food, some of which was not even meant for human consumption, in an undignified manner, the Hearst empire attempted to discredit and disprove the example we intended to display.

Thirdly, by prolonging the program, soliciting donations, and giving nowhere near the required amount, the Hearst empire could retain control under the facade of humanitarianism with no loss to their bank books.

The tactics of misplaced supply of the food, delayed and missing trucks, supposed hijackings of mysterious trucks claimed to be loaded with top-quality meat, are all designed to mislead the people into believing that these things were normal mishaps and that the Hearst empire was not responsible for them and was really attempting to meet some of the needs of the people.

The Hearst empire has attempted to encourage division among the people by giving them crumbs to fight over.

Our strategy was to show by example what can be done: That this goodwill gesture was intended to give some food to the people, while at the same time point out our understanding that the people can never expect the enemy to feed them. That, in fact, the people do not want the enemy to feed them, but rather the people must have back the land and control over their own destiny and must themselves realize the fruits of their own labor.

We did this to point out how the enemy can easily afford to feed the people if it were forced to, but what the enemy cannot afford is to reveal to the people the total extent of the sum of the wealth that it has robbed from the people.

The SLA stated that Patricia Campbell Hearst would be kept in accordance with international codes of war regarding prisoners of war, and that she would be maintained in protective custody. It was further stated that the captive SLA elements who stay at San Quentin would also have to be kept in accordance with such codes because of their legal POW status.

The SLA requested that Randolph and Catherine Hearst and the Hearst empire see to it that our comrades' conditions follow those guidelines. It was stated at that time that Patricia Hearst's condition would correspond at all times with that of the captured brothers. The SLA has waited with disciplined patience for the agents of the fascist state, including the Hearst media empire, to deal with the conditions of our comrades' confinement.

The Symbionese War Council, the Court of the People, had considered transferring Patricia Campbell Hearst to a security area which would physically correspond to a strip cell on death row in San Quentin concentration camp. This would be an obvious response to barbaric conditions which our comrades are forced to endure.

However, after extensive nationwide intelligence and analysis by the Symbionese War Council, it became clear that the fascist corporate state and its chief domestic police agency, the FBI, and other police state agencies and institutions, intended to set up Patricia Hearst for execution in order to discredit and isolate the people's forces.

This is shown by the deliberate disregard for the health, life, and safety of Joseph Remiro and Russell Little, and the plans of police state agencies to see to it that Patricia Hearst is killed.

Despite FBI claims that they would not do anything to endanger Patricia Hearst's life, they have raided homes throughout the country knowing full well that to do so would endanger the life of Patricia Hearst.

The plans of the police state agency are to see to it that Patricia Hearst is killed and then use her death to further rally middle America in support of the Nixon-represented corporate dictatorship and against all revolutionary forces.

The fascist state and the FBI have attempted to manipulate public opinion in support of Patricia Hearst's safety and eventual return while at the same time create conditions that it knows would force her execution, saving them the embarrassment of doing it themselves.

But we have repeatedly stated that Patricia Hearst's safety, execution, or freedom is totally her family's and its class's responsibility.

It is in the direct interest of the fascist corporate state to eliminate all popular revolutionary forces, even if that would mean sending the FBI to execute Patricia Hearst.

U.S. Attorney General William Saxbe's statement that the FBI should bust in to rescue the prisoner was no slip of the tongue, but was in reality a prematurely exposed government policy decision.

Just as Nelson Rockefeller and the prison authorities in New York State could easily sacrifice the lives of hostage correctional officers at Attica in order to kill incarcerated freedom fighters inside, just as Ronald Reagan and prison authorities in California could sacrifice the life of Judge Haley at the Marin County Courthouse in order to kill manchild Jonathan Jackson and incarcerated freedom fighters from San Quentin, so, too, can the U.S. government and the FBI, with the sick permission of her father, willingly and without regret sacrifice the life of Patricia Hearst in order to attempt to kill members of the Symbionese Liberation Army.

We know from our experiences in prisons, and from our comrades who have been killed in prisons, and from all those comrades still locked down, that Russell Little and Joseph Remiro have already been issued tickets to ride the fascist corporate state's railroad to the gas chamber, and that the appointment by Randolph Hearst of a member of the fascist UC Board of Regents to ensure so-called due process of law is merely a ploy to hide the already predetermined destination of that train, not to stop it.

In response to Randolph Hearst's public request that Patricia Hearst be allowed to communicate periodically with her family in conjunction with international codes of war regarding prisoners of war, the SLA asks Randolph Hearst: On what basis should the people's forces allow such communications?

First, the Symbionese War Council has determined that communication between POW Patricia Hearst and her family will come after the immediate creation of the necessary mechanisms whereby Russell Little and Joseph Remiro can communicate via live national TV with the people and the SLA concerning the full scope of their physical health and all the conditions of their confinement.

Second, that this tape and a transcript of it be published in full, omitting nothing, in all forms of the media.

the voice of Patricia Hearst

Mom, Dad, I received the message you broadcast last Sunday. It was good to hear from you after so much silence, but what you had to say sounded like you don't care if I ever get out of here. All you want is to hear from me sometimes. Your silence definitely jeopardized my safety because it allows the FBI to continue to attempt to find me, and Governor Reagan to make antagonistic statements, with no response from you.

I'm beginning to feel that the FBI would rather that I get killed than safely released. I'm telling you this now because I don't believe the FBI will let any more words from me get through to the media. I hear that people all around the country keep calling on the SLA to release me unharmed. But the SLA are not the ones who are harming me. It's the FBI, along with your indifference to the poor, and your failure to deal with people and the SLA in a really sincere manner.

I don't believe that you're doing everything you can, everything in your power. I don't believe that you're doing anything at all. You said that it was out of your hands; what you should have said was that you wash your hands of it.

I guess that you don't understand that it is not just the crimes of you and Mom personally that I am being held for, but the crimes of the University of California Board of Regents, and your voting record, Mom, when you were on that board. And also the crimes of the Hearst Corporation.

Dad, you say you put responsibility for my status on the corporation, but you seem to be ignoring the fact that you are the chairman of the board and Uncle Bill is president of the Hearst Corporation. I know that if anything happens to me, it will be because your corporation adviser and the FBI decided to protect their interests instead of my life.

I don't know who influenced you to not comply with the good-faith gesture. I know you could have done it the way the SLA asked. I mean I know that we have enough money. But it seems to me that you told the FBI to do whatever they decide is necessary to destroy the SLA. This is really true, Dad.

I've heard the reports concerning the FBI investigation and interrogations, Governor Reagan's careless and antagonistic remarks, and the attempts of federal agencies and the use of the news media to mentally prepare the public for my death, by calling for mass prayers and petitions to the SLA for my release.

From this I am forced to draw only one conclusion, that the FBI and other federal agencies want me to die. I no longer seem to have any importance as a human being; rather, I have become all-important as a political pivot point for certain right-wing elements, and I can only be used successfully by these people if I am killed.

As for the constant reassurances by the FBI that my safety is their primary concern, I can only say that the FBI has never been famous for its concern for the safety of hostages, and from what I've seen so far this case is no different.

Whether consciously or not, the news media has been assisting the FBI in its now overt attempts to set me up for execution. It has done this primarily in two ways.

First, by promoting a public image of my father as a bereaved parent who has done all he can to meet the demands of his daughter's kidnappers, and who now awaits her supposedly long overdue release. In fact, the SLA demands have not even been approximated, and they have made it very clear that until the good-faith gesture is completed, negotiations for my release will not begin.

Second, the media, with cooperation from my parents, has created a public image of me as a helpless innocent girl who was supposedly abducted by two terrible black escaped convicts. I'm a strong woman and I resent being used in this way.

I have been hearing reports about the food program. So far it sounds like you and your advisors have managed to turn it into a real disaster.

I heard that only fifteen thousand people received food in the first two weeks and that each of them received only about eight dollars' worth. It sounds like most of the food is of low quality. No one received any beef or lamb. Anyway, it certainly didn't sound like the kind of food our family is used to eating.

The SLA wanted this program to be over in one month. They wanted each person to get seventy dollars' worth of good food all at once. If you had just done what the SLA wanted for the food program, the month would be almost over and I would be ready to get out of here.

What you've done is tell People in Need to set up this program where people get just an eight-dollar bag of food, so it's being stretched out into a really discouraging thing for the people who need food.

Dad, I know that you got most of the food donated to People in Need and that you have put very little money at all into the program.

Mom, I can't believe that you agreed with the "out of my hands" stance that Dad has taken. I just wish that you could be stronger and pull yourself together from all these emotional outbursts and see if you can persuade Dad to listen to you and the rest of the family. Mom, you've got to stand up and speak for yourself. You seem to be allowing other people to make your decisions.

Your statements, if I can call them that, have given the FBI the go-ahead to kill me. I wish God would touch your heart and get you to do something concrete to help me.

I wish I knew what the rest of the family was thinking and saying. It's hard to believe that my sisters and cousins aren't saying anything.

If it had been you, Mom, or you, Dad, who had been kidnapped instead of me, I know that I and the rest of the family and your friends would do anything to get you back. It could have been one of you and how would you feel if you had been written off the way I seem to have been?

I'm starting to think that no one is concerned about me anymore. I wish that I could hear from the rest of the family. I'd like to hear what my sisters have to say about Dad's decision not to comply with the terms of the good-faith gesture.

Steven, what do you have to say? Willy, I know you really care about what happens to me. Make Dad let you talk. You can't be silent.

Everyone who hears this tape, I hope you will believe me and not think that I've been brainwashed or tortured into saying this. Please listen to me because I'm speaking honestly and from the heart.

In the last week it has become obvious to the SLA and all hungry people, and to me, that my father has not even attempted to show a gesture of good faith, and I guess everyone knows by now that that is why there's no further word from the SLA about negotiating for my release.

In the last few days, members of the Federation have spoken with me. They have given me some newspaper reports to read about the current practices of psychosurgery and the use of daily doses of drugs and tranquilizers in prisons throughout the country. I have also been given some journal commentaries about the kinds of conditions that exist in prisons in general and in the adjustment center at San Quentin in particular.

Members of the Federation have also given me a choice of books to read. I have been reading a book by George Jackson called *Blood in My Eye.* I'm starting to understand what he means when he talks about fascism in America.

Joseph Remiro and Russell Little, the two men in San Quentin, haven't even come to trial yet, and already they are being held in strip cells on death row. It's really hard to believe that such an obvious violation of the Constitution is taking place, but it's true. How can people think that these men can get a fair trial? Can there be any doubt in people's minds as to what the verdict will be?

Members of the Federation have shown me intelligence reports gathered by the SLA on the activities of the FBI. These, combined with discussions the members of the Federation have had with me, and my own observations of the way my father is conducting himself, have made me afraid because I realize that plans are coming from the FBI and the Attorney General's office in Washington to execute the two men in San Quentin. Or, if that cannot be swiftly accomplished, to execute me by seeing to it that even if I am released I will not get home alive. Or, by attempting to raid this place where I am being held, and then discredit the SLA by saying that they were the ones who killed me.

Because of these dangers, I have been transferred to a special security unit of the SLA combat forces, where I am being held in protective custody. I have been issued a twelve-gauge riot shotgun and I have been receiving instructions on how to use it.

While I have no access to ammunition, in the event of an attack by the FBI, I have been told that I will be given an issue of cyanide buckshot in order to protect myself because it is the Federation's opinion, and my own from observation, that if the

FBI does rush in, it will obviously be doing this against the wishes of my family and in total disregard for my safety. In fact, they would be doing it to murder me.

Under international codes of war I am allowed to communicate with members of my family and, because of the scope of this incident, with the public as well. However, I should tell you that the practice of allowing me to communicate with you will not continue until the SLA hears from the two men at San Quentin. They want to hear what the two men have to say in a live nationwide broadcast, so they can hear all the conditions of their confinement.

I really want to get out of here and I really want to get home alive. I am appealing to the public and asking them *not* to assist the FBI in their investigation. Doing so is simply helping them to dig my grave. I ask those people who say they pray for me and those who sign petitions to the SLA for my safe release to redirect their energies into opposing the FBI's brutal attempts to murder me and the two men in San Quentin.

I no longer fear the SLA, because they are not the ones who want me to die. The SLA want to feed the people, and assure safety and justice for the two men at San Quentin. I realize now it is the FBI who wants to murder me. Only the FBI and certain people in the government stand to gain anything by my death.

the voice of Angela Atwood (Gelina)

A warning to the fascist corporate military state:

We have declared revolutionary war upon you, the enemy of the people, and our seriousness and determination will not be swayed by any number of your U.S.-government-inspected super-pigs. For those that you have hunted are now hunting you.

Death to the fascist insect that preys upon the life of the people.

the voice of Nancy Ling Perry (Fahizah)

Comrade sisters, resistance fighters, we greet you and call you to arms in the struggle to free all people.

Today our daughters and our sons, our mothers and our fathers, stand with the people and fight for the true freedom for all people. No people are free until we are all free.

We women know the truth as it has been revealed in our own lives. We turn our rage toward the enemy in a direct line, down the sights of our guns. We must turn our anger towards those who profit off our suffering, and have our anger be reflected in military tactics that utilize people's violence against the men and women who are the monsters of capitalist violence.

Until we meet in the street may we have a strong back, like that of the gravedigger.

the voice of Donald DeFreeze (Cinque)

This is General Field Marshal Cinque in command. I would like to take the opportunity to speak to my people and to all the people, and to those that I fight beside against the enemy that preys upon the life of our children.

The time has come when we as black people must come together and stop robbing and oppressing each other and other oppressed people. It is time that black people understand that the enemy is not white, brown, or black people.

The oppressor is not a particular color. The oppressor is a system and the corporate ruling class that it represents that preys upon the life of all people.

I call upon oppressed people of all colors to arm themselves in defense of their own freedom while they still have the chance.

I call upon the robber, the pimp, the drug addict, the prostitute, and all those who have been used as pawns against the people, to turn their rage and violence towards the true enemy of the people, the corporate ruling class.

I call upon the people to shed no more blood of the innocent but rather bring death to the makers of fear, those that would deceive us into fighting amongst ourselves because of our different colors.

I call upon our mothers and fathers to hear the voice that rings in our hearts for freedom.

I call upon them to hear the cries of our children being murdered in the streets, and to understand that there is no compromise for freedom.

I call upon the people to join the Federation by the only means one can: that is, by answering this call to arms with the sounds of your guns and your commitment to save the children.

the voice of an unknown woman

This is Information Intelligence Unit Four. On March 9th, 1974, this unit was directed to deliver a taped communique to the news media. Due to intelligence reports received by the Federation in regards to FBI attempts to intercept and suppress any communications between the SLA and the people, a double-decoy system was set up.

One tape with a gasoline credit card was sent to radio station KDIA Oakland and another tape enclosed with an automobile credit card was sent to KSAN. We of Unit Four notified KDIA first as to the location of this tape, which allowed one of two things to happen:

Either KDIA, without telling the public or the Hearst family, turned it over to FBI who in turn suppressed it, keeping it from the Hearst family and public, or the FBI intercepted it before KDIA got it and suppressed it from getting to the Hearst family and the public.

In any event, this allowed the second tape to get through to KSAN, because the FBI thought that the tape they had already intercepted was the only one sent out.

We of Unit Four are sending our copy of the tape because it is more audible. Please pass it along.

March 25, 1974

The final People in Need food distribution occurs.

late March, 1974

The SLA leave Daly City and move to another safehouse, an apartment at 1827 Golden Gate Avenue in San Francisco.

CODES OF WAR
MARCH 29, 1974

This communication is to be sent through you to the people. You are hereby directed by the Court of the People to notify immediately radio stations KPFA, KSAN and KDIA concerning the complete contents of this communication, understanding that you must not cooperate with the FBI by turning over this communication or by providing them with any information.

Protect your rights as reporters by refusing to reveal your sources of information.

Communique No. 7
March 29, 1974
Symbionese Liberation Army, Information and Intelligence Unit No. 4
Court Order: Release of the Codes of War of the SLA. Court Order issued by the Court of the people.
Subject: negotiations and release of Prisoner.

Herein enclosed are the Codes of War of the Symbionese Liberation Army, these documents as all SLA documents are to be printed in full and omitting nothing by order of this court in all forms of the media. Further communications regarding subject prisoner will follow in the following 72 hours. Communications will state the state, city and time of release of the prisoner.

Signed: I.I. Unit 4

General Field Marshall Cin, SLA

CODES OF WAR OF THE UNITED SYMBIONESE LIBERATION ARMY

PENALTY BY DEATH

ALL CHARGES THAT FACE A DEATH PENALTY SHALL BE PRESENTED TO A JURY TRIAL MADE UP OF THE MEMBERS OF THE GUERRILLA FORCES. THE JURY SHALL BE SELECTED BY THE CHARGED AND THE JUDGE CONDUCTING THE TRIAL SHALL BE SELECTED BY THE CHARGED ALSO. THE CHARGED SHALL SELECT HIS OR HER DEFENSE, AND THE TRIAL JUDGE SHALL SELECT THE PROSECUTOR. THE JURY SHALL NUMBER AT LEAST 3/4THS OF THE REMAINING MEMBERS OF THE CELLS, AND THE VERDICT MUST BE UNANIMOUS.

1. THE SURRENDER TO THE ENEMY.
2. THE KILLING OF A COMRADE OR DISOBEYING ORDERS THAT RESULT IN THE DEATH OF A COMRADE.
3. THE DESERTING OF A COMRADE ON THE FIELD OF WAR.

   A. LEAVING A TEAM POSITION, THEREBY NOT COVERING A COMRADE.

   B. LEAVING A WOUNDED COMRADE.
4. THE INFORMING TO THE ENEMY OR SPYING

AGAINST THE PEOPLE OR GUERRILLAS.

5. LEAVING A CELL UNIT OR BASE CAMP WITHOUT ORDERS.

Any comrade may leave the guerrilla forces if she or he feels that they no longer feel the courage or faith in the people and the struggle that we wage. A comrade, however, must follow the codes of war in doing this: that is, he or she must inform the commanding guerrilla of their wish to go from the guerrilla force. Thereupon, the guerrilla in command will release them in a safe area. The excombatants may only leave with his or her personal side-arm. REMEMBER, this is the ONLY way a comrade may leave the S.L.A., any other way is deserting, punishable by death.

6. ALL PAID OR UNPAID INFORMANTS OPERATING WITHIN THE COMMUNITY AGAINST THE PEOPLE AND THE GUERRILLA FORCES ARE SENTENCED WITHOUT TRIAL TO IMMEDIATE DEATH.

PENALTY BY DISCIPLINARY ACTION

DISCIPLINARY ACTION SHOULD BE PRIMARILY TO AID THE COLLECTIVE GROWTH OF THE CELL SO THAT THROUGH POSITIVE ACTION THE MISTAKE IS UNDERSTOOD, ALL CHARGES THAT FACE DISCIPLINARY ACTION SHALL BE UNDER THE FULL CONTROL OF THE GUERRILLA IN COMMAND, AND SHE OR HE SHALL WEIGH ALL EVIDENCE AND SHALL DECIDE THE VERDICT, AND IF NEEDED, DIRECT. THE DISCIPLINARY ACTION TO BE TAKEN BY THE CHARGED COMRADE

NECESSARY TO DIRECT HIM OR HER. EXAMPLES OF DISCIPLINARY ACTION ARE: THE CLEANING AND MAINTENANCE OF ALL CELL ARMS, AMMUNITION AND EXPLOSIVES FOR ONE WEEK, THE UP KEEP OF OUTHOUSES, THE FULL SUSPENSION OF WINE AND CIGARETTES, AND EXTRA DUTIES SUCH AS ADDITIONAL WATCHES, PRACTICE AND STUDY PERIODS, CORRESPONDENCE, FILING, TYPING, WASHING, CLEANING, COOKING, AND PHYSICAL EXERCISES.

1. LACK OF RESPONSIBILITY AND DETERMINED DECISIVENESS IN FOLLOWING ORDERS.

2. NONVIGILANCE OR THE LEAVING OF AN ASSIGNED POST WITHOUT ORDERS.

3. LACK OF RESPONSIBILITY IN MAINTAINING EQUIPMENT OR PROFICIENCY IN ALL GUERRILLA SKILLS, ESPECIALLY SHOOTING.

4. THE USE OF ANY UNMEDICALLY PRESCRIBED DRUG.

THIS RULE RELATES TO THE USE OF SUCH DRUGS AS HEROIN, SPEED, PEYOTE, MESCALINE, REDS, PEP PILLS, WHITES, YELLOW JACKETS, BENNIES, DEXIES, GOOF BALLS, LSD, AND ANY OTHER KIND OF HALLUCINARY DRUGS. HOWEVER, PERMISSION IS GRANTED FOR THE USE OF ONLY TWO TYPES OF RELAXING DRUGS: THESE ARE MARIJUANA, AND/OR BEER AND WINE AND OTHER ALCOHOL. THIS PERMISSION IS ONLY GRANTED WHEN APPROVED BY THE GUERRILLA IN COMMAND, AND WITH VERY RESTRAINING USE ONLY. NO OFFICER MAY

GRANT THE USE OF ANY OF THESE SAID DRUGS TO THE FULL NUMBER OF FORCES UNDER HIS OR HER COMMAND. IF THIS PERMISSION IS GRANTED ONLY HALF THE FORCE WILL BE ALLOWED TO TAKE PART, WHILE THE OTHER HALF WILL STAND GUARD DUTY.

THE PAST HAS SHOWN ONCE TRUE REVOLUTIONARIES HAVE SERIOUSLY UNDERTAKEN REVOLUTIONARY ARMS STRUGGLE, MARIJUANA AND ALCOHOL ARE NOT USED FOR RECREATIONAL PURPOSES OR TO DILUTE OR BLUR THE CONSCIOUSNESS OF REALITY, BUT VERY SMALL AMOUNTS FOR MEDICINAL PURPOSES TO CALM NERVES UNDER TIMES OF TENSION, NOT TO DISTORT REALITY.

5. THE FAILURE TO SEVER ALL PAST CONTACTS OR FAILING TO DESTROY ALL EVIDENCE OF IDENTIFICATION OR ASSOCIATION.

6. KILLING OF AN UNARMED ENEMY: IN THIS INSTANCE THE ENEMY REFERS TO MEMBERS OF U.S.A. RANK AND FILE ONLY AND NOT TO ANY MEMBERS OF THE CIA, FBI, OR OTHER SPECIAL AGENTS OR ANY POLITICAL POLICE STATE AGENTS. MEMBERS OF THE USA MILITARY RANK AND FILE ARE TO BE ACCORDED THIS DISTINCTION BECAUSE WE RECOGNIZE THAT MANY OF THEM HAVE BEEN FORCED INTO MEMBERSHIP EITHER DIRECTLY, THROUGH THE DRAFT, OR INDIRECTLY DUE TO ECONOMIC PRESSURES.

7. TORTURES OR SEXUAL ASSAULT ON EITHER A COMRADE OR PEOPLE OF THE ENEMY.

8. CRIMINAL ACTS AGAINST THE POOR, COMRADES

OR GUERRILLA FORCES.

9. MALICIOUS CURSING OR ANY KIND OF DISRESPECT TO THOSE IN COMMAND, A COMRADE, OR THE PEOPLE.

10. DECEIVING OR LYING TO FELLOW COMRADES OR THE PEOPLE. IF ANY OF THESE ACTS ARE COMMITTED ON A CONTINUOUS BASIS, THE CHARGED COMRADE SHALL BECOME A PRISONER OF THE CELL AND SHALL REMAIN IN THIS PRISONER STATUS UNTIL SUCH TIME AS SHE OR HE IS ABLE TO PROVE THEIR RENEWED COMMITMENT TO REVOLUTIONARY DISCIPLINE AND REVOLUTIONARY PRINCIPLES OR THE CHARGED MAY REQUEST TO BE DISHONORABLY DISCHARGED.

CONDUCT OF GUERRILLA FORCES TOWARDS THE ENEMY SOLDIERS AND PRISONERS.

1. PRISONERS OF WAR SHALL BE HELD UNDER THE INTERNATIONAL CODES OF WAR, THEY SHALL BE PROVIDED WITH ADEQUATE FOOD, MEDICAL AID, AND EXERCISES.

2. ALL USA MILITARY RANK AND FILE FORCES SHALL BE ALLOWED TO SURRENDER UPON OUR CONDITIONS OF SURRENDER, AND THEREUPON THEY SHALL BE CAREFULLY SEARCHED AND INTERROGATED. ALL PRISONERS ARE TO RECEIVE INSTRUCTION ON THE GOALS OF SYMBIONESE LIBERATION ARMY, THEN RELEASED IN A SAFE AREA.

3. ALL WEAPONS, MEDICAL AND FOOD SUPPLIES,

MAPS, MILITARY EQUIPMENT AND MONEY ARE TO BE CONFISCATED AND TURNED INTO THE GUERRILLA IN CHARGE.

4. UNDER NO CONDITIONS SHALL ANY RANK AND FILE ENEMY SOLDIER BE RELIEVED OF HIS OR HER PERSONAL PROPERTY.

CONDUCT OF GUERRILLA FORCES TOWARDS THE PEOPLE

ALL GUERRILLA FORCES SHALL CONDUCT THEMSELVES IN A MANNER OF RESPECT TOWARD THE PEOPLE, AND SHALL WHEN ABLE AND SAFE TO DO SO, PROVIDE FOOD AND OTHER AID TO THE PEOPLE. THEY SHALL, WHEN POSSIBLE, INFORM THE PEOPLE OF THE GOALS OF THE UNITED SYMBIONESE FEDERATION AND ENCOURAGE OTHER WOMEN AND MEN TO JOIN OUR FORCES AND TO SERVE THE PEOPLE IN FIGHT FOR FREEDOM.

ALL COMRADES HAVE ONE MAIN RESPONSIBILITY, THAT IS TO STRUGGLE AND WIN AND STAND TOGETHER, SO NO COMRADE STANDS ALONE. ALL MUST LOOK OUT FOR EACH OTHER. ALL MUST AID THE OTHER BLACK, BROWN, RED, YELLOW, WHITE, MAN OR WOMAN, ALL OR NONE.

THIS DOCUMENT MAY CHANGE FROM TIME TO TIME, SO OFFICERS ARE REQUESTED TO FOLLOW THE CHANGES WITH DISCIPLINE.

TO THOSE WHO WOULD BEAR THE HOPES AND FUTURE OF THE PEOPLE LET THE VOICE OF THEIR GUNS EXPRESS THE WORD OF FREEDOM.

Gen. Field Marshall
S.L.A.
Cin

March 31, 1974

Patricia Hearst takes off her blindfold and is accepted as a "comrade" of the Symbionese Liberation Army.

IN THE BELLY OF THE FASCIST BEAST
APRIL 3, 1974

[transcript of audio tape]

[a Polaroid photograph of Patricia Hearst posing as "Tania" with a gun in front of the SLA flag is enclosed with the tape]

the voice of Patricia Hearst (Tania)

To those who would bear the hopes and future of our people, let the voice of their guns express the words of freedom.

I would like to begin this statement by informing the public that I wrote what I am about to say. It's what I feel. I have never been forced to say anything on any tape. Nor have I been brainwashed, drugged, tortured, hypnotized, or in any way confused. As George Jackson wrote, "It's me, the way I want it, the way I see it."

Mom, Dad, I would like to comment on your efforts to supposedly secure my safety. The People in Need giveaway was a sham. You attempted to deceive the people, the SLA, and me in statements about your concern for myself and the people. You were playing games, stalling for time, time which the FBI was using in their attempts to assassinate me and the SLA elements which guarded me. You continued to report that you did everything in your power to pave the way for negotiations for my release. I hate to believe that you could have been so unimaginative as not to have even considered getting Little and Remiro released on bail.

While it was repeatedly stated that my conditions would at all times correspond with those of the captured soldiers, when your own lawyer went to inspect the hole at San Quentin, he approved the deplorable conditions there, another move which potentially jeopardized my safety. My mother's acceptance of the appointment to a second term as a UC regent, as you well knew, would have caused my immediate execution had the SLA been less than together about their political goals. Your actions have taught me a great lesson, and in a strange kind of way, I'm grateful to you.

Steven, I know that you are beginning to realize that there is no such thing as neutrality in time of war. There can be no compromise, as your experience with the FBI must have shown you. You have been harassed by the FBI because of your supposed connections with so-called radicals, and some people have even gone so far as to suggest that I arranged my own arrest. We both know what really came down that Monday night, but you don't know what's happened since then. I've changed, grown. I've become conscious and can never go back to the life we led before. What I'm saying may seem cold to you and to my old friends, but love doesn't mean the same thing to me anymore. My love has expanded as a result of my experiences to embrace all people. It's grown into an unselfish love for my comrades here, in prison, and on the streets. A love that comes from the knowledge that "no one is free until we are all free." While I wish that you could be a comrade, I don't expect it. All I expect is that you try to understand the changes I've gone through.

I have been given the choice of one, being released in a safe area, or two, joining the forces of the Symbionese Liberation Army and fighting for my freedom and the freedom of all oppressed people. I have chosen to stay and fight. One thing which I have learned is that the corporate ruling class will do anything in their power in order to maintain their position of control over the masses, even if this means the sacrifice of one of their own. It should be obvious that people who don't even care about their own children couldn't possibly care about anyone else's children. The things which are precious to these people are their money and power, and they will never willingly surrender either. People should not have to humiliate themselves by standing in lines in order to be fed, nor should they have to live in fear for their lives and the lives of their children, as Tyrone Guyton's mother will sadly attest to.

Dad, you said that you were concerned with my life, and you also said that you were concerned with the life and interests of all oppressed people in this country, but you are a liar in both areas and, as a member of the ruling class, I know for sure that yours and Mom's interests are never the interests of the people. Dad, you said that you would see about getting more job opportunities for the people, but why haven't you warned the people what's going to happen to them, that actually the few jobs they still have will be taken away?

You, a corporate liar, of course will say that you don't know what I'm talking about, but I ask you then to prove it, tell the poor and oppressed people of this nation what the corporate state is about to do, warn black and poor people that they are about to be murdered down to the last man, woman, and child. If you're so interested in the people, why don't you tell them what the energy crisis really is. Tell them how it's nothing more than a manufactured strategy, a way of hiding industry's real intentions. Tell the people that the energy crisis is nothing more than a means to get public approval for a massive program to build nuclear power plants all over the nation.

Tell the people that the entire corporate state is, with the aid of this massive power supply, about to totally automate the entire industrial state, to the point that in the next five years all that will be needed will be a small class of button pushers. Tell the people, Dad, that all of the lower class and at least half of the middle class will be unemployed in the next three years, and that the removal of expendable excess, the removal of unneeded people, has already started. I want you to tell the people the truth. Tell them how the law-and-order programs are just a means to remove so-called violent, meaning aware, individuals from the community in order to facilitate the controlled removal of unneeded labor forces from this country, in the same way that Hitler controlled the removal of the Jews from Germany.

I should have known that if you and the rest of the corporate state were willing to do this to millions of people to maintain power and to serve your needs, you would also kill me if necessary to serve those same needs. How long will it take before white people in this country understand that whatever happens to a black child happens sooner or later to a white child? How long will it be before we all understand that we must fight for our freedom?

I have been given the name Tania after a comrade who fought

alongside Che in Bolivia for the people of Bolivia. I embrace the name with the determination to continue fighting with her spirit. There is no victory in half-assed attempts at revolution. I know Tania dedicated her life to the people, fighting with total dedication and an intense desire to learn, which I will continue in the oppressed American people's revolution. All colors of string in the web of humanity yearn for freedom!

Osceola and Bo,[†] even though we've never met, I feel like I know you. Timing brought me to you and I'm fighting with your freedom and the freedom of all prisoners in mind. In the strenuous jogs that life takes, you are pillars of strength to me. If I'm feeling down, I think of you, of where you are and why you are there, and my determination grows stronger. It's good to see that your spirits are so high in spite of the terrible conditions. Even though you aren't here, you are with other strong comrades, and the three of us are learning together, I in an environment of love and you in one of hate, in the belly of the fascist beast. We have grown closer to the people and become stronger through our experiences. I have learned how vicious the pig really is, and our comrades are teaching me to attack with even greater viciousness, in the knowledge that the people will win. I send greetings, to Death Row Jeff, Al Taylor, and Raymond Scott [prisoners]. Your concern for my safety is matched by my concern for yours. We share a common goal as revolutionaries knowing that comrade George lives.

It is in the spirit of Tania that I say, *"Patria o muerte, venceremos."*[‡]

[†] Imprisoned SLA members Russell Little and Joseph Remiro.

[‡] A quote from Fidel Castro – it translates as "Nation or death, we shall triumph."

the voice of William Harris (Teko)

Greetings to the people. My name is Teko. I am a white revolutionary and a soldier in the Symbionese Liberation Army. I have a message for all my white brothers who have not yet come forward to fight for the freedom of all oppressed people.

Contrary to what many of us may think, the special privileges white men as a group have gained for themselves through the oppression of all other people has never secured for us the freedom we desire. White men must understand that they will live under the threat of death as long as they continue to oppress the members of any class or group who have the strength and determination to fight back. White men themselves have only one avenue to freedom, and that is to join in fighting to the death those who are and those who aspire to be the slave masters of the world.

Many of us have been bold enough to intellectualize about revolution, but far too chickenshit to get down and help make it. Most of us have been nearly fatally stricken with the vile sickness of racism. Again, most of us have been immobilized by our sexist egos and have watched and done nothing as our sisters have rushed by us into battle. We have fooled ourselves into believing that Madison Avenue piggery will bring us eternal bourgeois happiness. If we haven't bought into the racist, sexist, capitalist, imperialist program, we have greened-out in Mendocino and New Hampshire. To black people, who lead our struggle to freedom, we have proved to be the racist punks of the world when we kick back and live off the blood and lives of the people.

However, many of us have seen through this sham and are fighting beside comrades from all races and classes, women and men, old and young. We know we have a long way to go to purify our minds of the many bourgeois poisons, but we also know that this isn't done through bullshitting and ego tripping, it is done by fighting and, as the comrade has taught us, by stalking the pig, seizing him by the tusks, and riding his pig ass into his grave. It is done by unleashing the most devastating revolutionary violence ever imagined, by proving that all races and groups of people can unite and fight together for the true freedom of us all.

When we call on the people to join us in the fight for freedom, many of you wonder how you can join the Symbionese Liberation Army, feeling that joining materially with those who are already fighting will provide the security you need to justify risking your lives. But we soldiers in the SLA say to this mistaken reasoning that you must read again our Declaration of Revolutionary War and Terms of Military Political Alliance. The SLA came into being because many people refused to wait for so-called revolutionary groups and organizations to lead them into a revolution which would, therefore, never come. We grew tired of waiting for mythological North American revolutionaries with the necessary expertise and skills we lack to teach us.

We have learned much from many brave revolutionary women and men, but in reality we are fighting today because we ourselves have seized the moment, taught ourselves, developed incredible strength, determination, and committed ourselves to never compromise with the enemy. As anyone with the most primitive of revolutionary mentalities knows, the people will not be given their freedom, they will have to seize it. Wait for no one, my brothers.

Death to the fascist insect that preys upon the life of the people.

the voice of Angela Atwood (Gelina)

Up until now, the fascist media has printed our documents in full because of their invested interest in Patricia Hearst. From now on, however, since this pressure point no longer exists, the fascist corporate military state, via the media, will lie about and distort any information concerning the SLA.

They will do this, one, in retaliation for being put in a position that required them to print everything, two, to try to isolate us from the people, and three, to discourage the people from joining the forces. Therefore, the people must watch and listen with keen perception. We will speak to you through action. Analyze these actions carefully, making sure to recognize when the enemy is in the disguise of revolutionaries. They will do anything to stop the rising of the people, including killing their own kind and blaming the people's forces under the pretense of a race war.

Remember that the SLA was born from the spirit of the people. The SLA is the people's army, and we fight in their interests. The SLA will never compromise. The SLA will not allow the enemy jive to deceive us into passively accepting genocide.

Listen and watch, and let that spirit become your name.

the voice of Nancy Ling Perry (Fahizah)

Love to our sisters and brothers in prisons. Courage and faith to our two captured soldiers. Greetings to all oppressed peoples, may we connect. My name is Fahizah.

The SLA is taking these opportunities to speak with the people now, because we have been having a temporary period of inactivity while waiting for the completion of our unit's last action. We know that the people want far more than six million dollars of food, and we will continue to fight for the total liberation of all oppressed peoples by the only means available, that is force of arms. The Court of the People has issued The Codes of War of the Symbionese Liberation Army, and I wish to state that Cinque Mtume is the General Field Marshal of the Symbionese Guerrilla Forces, as well as chairman of the United Symbionese War Council.

Cinque is a black brother who spent many years of his life in fascist America's concentration camps: manchild years in prison cells and man years in prison cells. Cinque met literally thousands of black, brown, red, yellow, and white freedom fighters while he was locked down. Courageous comrade George Jackson was one among them. The spirit of all the brothers Cinque knows lives in him now, and the spirit of all the sisters that Cinque never had the opportunity to meet but knows by common bond, like Assata Shakur, Lolita Lebrón, and Bernardine Dohrn,[†] is always in his heart.

When Cinque escaped alone on foot from Soledad prison, he did so for one reason only: to fight with the people and to lead the people in revolution. He did not escape so that he could kick back and hide and get high. He did not even escape so that he could satisfy a deep and longing personal ache to simply see the people, and be on the streets and reunite with his family and be a father once again to his children. Cinque escaped so that he could actively stalk the fascist insect that preys upon the life of the people. The lives both he and the people's fighting forces lead

[†] Assata Shakur of the Black Liberation Army, Lolita Lebrón of the Puerto Rican Nationalist Party, and Bernardine Dohrn of the Weather Underground.

now may be harsh and dangerous, but it is better to work with hard reality than to play in pleasant, but unproductive, enslaving dreams.

Cinque Mtume is the name that was bestowed upon him by his imprisoned sisters and brothers. It is the name of an ancient African chief who led the fight of his people for freedom. The name means Fifth Prophet, and Cin was many years ago given this name because of his keen instinct and senses, his spiritual consciousness, and his deep love for all the people and children of this earth. This does not, however, mean that Cinque is from God or someone that is holy or that he has an extreme ego problem, but simply that he, to us and to all oppressed peoples, is the instilled hope and spirit of his people and all peoples, and that he is of the people and from the people. A prophet is a leader and a fighter who is one of the people. Leaders are individuals who within themselves feel that it is time to lead and bring us one step closer to freedom for all peoples. A leader is one who is able to sense and to see what is coming at us. A leader is one who is able to help the people understand the swiftness and fierceness with which they must move if they would survive.

Part of the revolutionary process in which we are engaged involves the constant redefining of thought, word, and action. We must deal with all the conditions outside ourselves which oppress and enslave us, and we must deal with the enemy within. We must deal with both these diseases simultaneously, and with an unrelenting commitment and understanding that in reality we are not living to die, but rather all who choose to fight to the death are dying to live. Cin's example to the people has taught us, through his actions and by his own words, that he or she who is scared and seeks to run from death will find it, but she or he who is not afraid and who actively seeks death out will find it not at their door.

We embrace the concepts of art and spiritual consciousness in material relevant terms based upon the common conditions of all oppressed peoples. We have begun to redefine art as the natural creative reflection of our desperate struggle to survive. Art for us is the total process of sharing and communally using what we learn in order to live and to fight. We recognize Cin as an artist for what he teaches the people, but we also realize, as he himself has said, that truth has no author. Another thing which we feel is necessary to clarify is the word *spirit* and all that which is called *spiritual*. The spirit is the bodies and souls of all the people, and the spiritual is the intensity of our common instincts, as reflected throughout history, to fight for the freedom of all oppressed peoples, to save the earth and the children from the putrid disease of bourgeois mentality and the putrid disease of the corporate fascist military state. In a profound and spiritual sense, as our sisters and brothers in the BLA[†] have said, resistance to this disease is the single greatest human endeavor today.

Comrades in struggle, there is a high price that we have paid and will pay for our mistakes, and there is an even higher price which we have been paying for the loss of our leaders. We are speaking to the people now, because we all know that we cannot afford the loss of another leader, and we want the people to know that in spite of the enemy's technology and prestige of terror, we do have a leader that loves the people, and lives and fights for the people. This example helps to make a love among

[†] The Black Liberation Army.

comrades that gives attention, appreciation, care, and protection from each brother and sister to the other.

The oppressed peoples of this nation have and will continue to bring forth their leaders, prophets, and fighters until they are free. The people brought forth Malcolm X, who came to unite the people and warn the enemy of what would inevitably happen if the people were not freed. The enemy answered by murdering Malcolm. The people then did again bring forth another prophet, that prophet was Martin Luther King, who with nonviolence and humanity pleaded to the enemy to free the people. And just when King was ready to declare that nonviolent protest would accomplish nothing but the further enslavement and degradation of the people, the enemy murdered King. George Jackson was a prophet and leader from the streets, and when the enemy imprisoned him, George received his education in the raw. He learned firsthand that there can be no compromise with merciless pigs. George Jackson came from the prisons of America and, love-inspired, he boldly fought the oppressor. When the fascist insect locked him down and murdered him, the people knew that they had suffered a great loss, but they failed to unite in immediate retaliation. Now, once again, the people have brought forth another prophet and leader.

This leader comes not to beg and plead with the enemy, he comes not to warn of violence, but is himself the bringer of the children of the wind and the sound of war. He has one word to the children of the oppressed and the children of the oppressor: *come.* We have joined together with love and unity and the understanding that those who would be free must themselves strike the first blow.

the voice of Donald DeFreeze (Cinque)

This is Field Marshal Cin. I would like to take this opportunity on behalf of the Federation to thank WAPAC and all the other coalition members for their aid in feeding and educating the people. We send you our faith and unity to always serve the people.

I wish to say to those who will speak about what they want, to you I say that your words and cries will bring you nothing but a wet face and an empty heart. The enemy is unhearing and he is unmerciful to the oppressed. If you would have freedom for your children and the people, then you as a all-oppressed people will have to fight and struggle for it. Freedom is not tax deductible, nor is it willed to you. No piece of paper can sign it over to you or your children, it is something that in a oppressive world can only be gained and protected by the force of your arms and your spirit to defend that freedom at any cost.

To the people and combat forces of the people, business of the revolution:

The following are enemies of the people. They are agents of the enemy and have been found guilty of working and informing to the enemy against the people, and therefore death warrants have been issued by this court against them, and they should be shot on sight by any of the people's forces when found.

Robyn Steiner,[†] female, white, age twenty, hazel eyes, brown hair, height five four, wears contact lenses, a hundred and fifteen pounds, past resident of Berkeley, now living in Florida, informer to the FBI.

[†] Imprisoned SLA member Russell Little's girlfriend.

Chris Thompson,[†] male, black, brown eyes, brown hair, slender build, six three, Berkeley resident, is a government agent and paid informer for the FBI.

Colston Westbrook,[‡] male, black, age thirty-five, brown eyes, brown hair, height five eight, two hundred and ten pounds in weight, Berkeley language instructor, resident of Oakland, is a government agent, worked for the CIA in Vietnam as the interrogator and torturer in the Phoenix operation against the Vietnamese people, and also served same purpose in other foreign countries, now working for military intelligence while giving cross-assistance to the FBI.

These subjects are to be shot on sight whenever found at any time.

Concerning the Hearst operation:

The government dictatorship, as well as the Hearst empire, has shown that they are quite willing to murder even their own to maintain power over the people, therefore it is the judgment of this court that in the future no prisoners of the ruling class or its executive agents will be taken prisoner. The Court of the People this date issues the following order: All corporate enemies of the people will be *shot* on sight at any time and at any place. This order is permanent, until such time as all enemy forces have either surrendered or been destroyed.

Concerning the protective-custody prisoner:

The subject has been freed but has refused to go home or take part as a member of the enemy fascist state. There is no further

[†] An SLA friend who cooperated with police after one of his registered guns was used in the Marcus Foster assassination.

[‡] The Black Cultural Association "outside coordinator" at Vacaville.

need to discuss the release of the prisoner under this condition, since the prisoner is now a comrade and has been accepted into the ranks of the people's army as a comrade and fighter for the people's freedom, and therefore there is no further basis for negotiations since the subject may leave whenever she feels that she wishes to do. She is armed and well capable to defend herself. This operation is hereby terminated and suspension of offensive operations is hereby rescinded, and all combat forces of the SLA and all people's forces are requested and so ordered to resume normal offensive combat operations against all enemies of the people. The Court of the People wishes to note that the people do not wish to be fed by the rich, the people want back the land.

To our two soldiers who are in the hands of the enemy and to all our comrades behind the walls:

As you know, we have learned a hard lesson from our mistakes and will learn from this for the future and the war that we the people will win. I am sure that you understand that under our codes of war there can be no surrender to the enemy, at any time or at any place. You both have shown correct actions in recognizing that, even though you are innocent of any crimes, it is not possible for you to receive a fair trial in the enemy's arena. I deeply regret that you were not offensively prepared to attack rather than be seized by the enemy. I send you my love and the love of all of your comrades, and courage in your determination to carry on the struggle even from that side of the wall, as we will never relent from this side. In this way we do expect to meet again.

At this point, I would like to take the opportunity to speak to my six lovely black babies: Victor, Damon, Sherry, Sherlyne,

Dawn, and Dede. I want you to know that to just say your names again fills my heart with joy. I want you to know that I love you all with all the love that a father can have for those so dear to him, and I want you to understand also that I have not forgotten my promise to you, that whenever you needed me, I would be there at your side, and so I am now even when you may not see me, I am there, because no matter where I am, I am fighting for your freedom, your future, and your life. Daddy wants you to understand that I can't come home because you and the people are not free, and, as long as the enemy exists, I can find no rest nor any hope for you or our people as a whole. I can't be happy when the enemy murders the children of other fathers and mothers. I want you to understand that I have to fight for you and for all fathers and mothers who must stay home, or who have not the courage to fight, or the clear understanding yet that the greatest gift they can give their children is freedom.

To you, my children, even when I may never see you again, know that I love you and will not for any price forsake your freedom and the freedom of all oppressed people. To you I give all that a father could wish, I give you life without fear and exploitation, I give you love with a future, understanding that the price of freedom is daring to struggle, daring to win. In ending this letter to you, I ask only one thing of you all, that you promise me that you will always honor the people and love the children and defend them both at any price against any enemy.

In closing I wish to play the national anthem of the Symbionese Liberation Army.†

† The instrumental song "Way Back Home" by The Crusaders begins to play in the background.

My people, my brothers, my sisters, free the people, free the land, and save the children.

April 4, 1974

Randolph and Catherine Hearst, exhausted, fly to Mexico to recuperate at the house of their friend Desi Arnaz.

early April, 1974

The San Francisco Police Department begins to issue "Zebra Check" cards to black men to record that they have been profiled, detained, and cleared in relation to the Zebra killings. A U.S. district court judge rules that the profiling is unconstitutional after over five hundred black men are issued cards.

April 15, 1974

Five members of the SLA – Donald DeFreeze, Nancy Ling Perry, Camilla Hall, Patricia Mizmoon Soltysik, and newly recruited Patricia Hearst – rob the Sunset-area branch of Hibernia Bank in San Francisco; William Wolfe, Angela Atwood, and William and Emily Harris wait in a nearby getaway car. Two male bystanders suffer minor gunshot wounds, and the bank robbery is recorded on film. A total of $10,692.51 in cash is stolen.

YOUR TIME IS RUNNING SHORT

APRIL 22, 1974

[transcript of audio tape]

the voice of Donald DeFreeze (Cinque)

To those who would bear the hopes and future of our people, let the voice of their guns express the words of freedom.

Greetings to the people and all sisters and brothers behind the walls and in the streets. To units of the Black Liberation Army, the Weather Underground and the Black Guerrilla Family, and all combat forces of the community. This is General Field Marshal Cin speaking.

Combat operation: April 15th, 1974, the year of the children.

Action: Appropriation.

Supplies liberated: One .38 Smith and Wesson revolver, condition good. Five rounds of 158-grain .30-caliber ammo. Cash: $10,660.02.

Number of rounds fired by combat forces: Seven rounds.

Number of rounds lost: Five.

Casualties: People's forces, none. Enemy forces, none. Civilian, two.

Reasons: Subject one, male. Subject was ordered to lay on the floor face down. Subject refused order and jumped out the front door of the bank. Therefore the subject was shot. Subject two, male. Subject failed or did not hear warning to clear the street. Subject was running down the street towards the bank, and combat forces accordingly assumed subject was a armed enemy-force element. Therefore the subject was shot.

We again warn the public. Any civilian attempting to aid, to inform, or to assist the enemy of the people in any manner will be shot without hesitation. There is no middle ground in war. Either you are the people or the enemy. *You* must make the choice.

As a black man and a father and as representative of black people, I would like to say that I, as well as many other black people, have been watching the actions taken against black people over in the city of San Francisco, and also in Berkeley and Oakland, by the racist agents of the ruling class.

Like most of my people, I never trust anything the enemy says or does. I must at all time be suspicious or discount any acts on his part as not being what they first seem to be. Following this principle, I must look at the so-called Zebra operation with more attention, since it is an action against the freedom of the people.

For the love that I hold for the people drive myself and all the SLA to understand that we must fight and defend the people.

I at first had thought that Operation Zebra was really nothing more than a normal counterinsurgency operation to attempt to entrap the SLA forces, and more precisely to assassinate myself. I say assassinate because the enemy knows by now who I am and the danger that I represent as long as I am alive.

He understands that if he can terrorize and disarm the black community with some action adjoining me, then he will be able to isolate me specifically and to kill me, thereby not allowing me the time to educate men and women from the communities to become leaders of our people.

He also understands that I have been bringing the children of the oppressed and the children of the oppressor together. He understands that I am bringing the truth to the children and opening their eyes to the real enemy of humanity by simply allowing them to see the enemy as he truly is, and allowing them to find out really who the people are, and that the people love them and will welcome them with open arms if they will just come.

In short, he knows that the SLA is building an army of the people. That is the army which by its very composition can truly destroy the enemy and free the people.

At this point, I am more inclined to feel, however, that Operation Zebra is a lot more than just entrapping the SLA. In fact, I feel the enemy knows that he or she can never totally entrap all the SLA forces, regardless of the size of the city in which counterinsurgency operations may take place. Reports that units and bases of the SLA are under surveillance by the FBI is designed to demoralize the people and attempt to make them believe in the prestige of the enemy.

In any event, understanding these points we come back again to the same question: What is Operation Zebra? If Operation Zebra is not merely a counterinsurgency operation, then what is it? And, if we look closely, we begin to see the truth that Operation Zebra is a planned enemy offensive against the people to create a race war. This could possibly be the only way the enemy can stop the SLA from bringing all oppressed people together against the common enemy.

Operation Zebra is even more than that. The so-called Zebra killer will never be found, because it is the only justification, notwithstanding martial law being declared, whereby the enemy can stop and arrest any black male. In fact we can expect, in the next few months, under the guise of searching for the so-called Zebra killer, block-by-block and house-by-house searches. And of course all weapons found in the people's homes will be confiscated under the guise of stolen property or that they have to be verified as not being the murder weapon. In short, the people will be disarmed.

Operation Zebra serves yet even another purpose of the enemy. It is a means to remove as many black males from the community as possible, at the same time pressing all of the black males to submit to FBI classification and identification, which is being applied in the form of so-called police passes, by using each person's driver's license and Social Security card numbers, which are, I may mention, key codes for the FBI's computer systems.

Now people, I warn you again: The only way, I repeat, the only way you will regain your life and freedom is to fight.

The only way you will keep your guns is to use them.

Your time is running short. Open your eyes.

Death to the fascist insect that preys upon the life of the people.

the voice of William Harris (Teko)

Greetings to the people. This is Teko speaking.

As it has been stated many times by the black community, the Zebra operation is a planned enemy offensive against the people to create a race war. Race war is a fascist tactic to divide the people. The pigs know that there is no way to control or eliminate the people's army.

The people's army in the United States of America means a guerrilla force of black, brown, red, yellow, and white people united by their fighting spirit and their common determination to kill the pig. The Symbionese Liberation Army is a people's army, and the only way the fascists can slow us down is to try to scare the people into fighting among themselves.

The pigs and the fascist media have, by their slick trickery, attempted to link the SLA with the so-called Zebra killings. They have even gone so far as to release a composite drawing and description of the killer which has the resemblance to General Field Marshal Cinque Mtume. The next lie that we expect to hear is that Cinque is the Zebra killer, and this will be to give even greater pig justification to continue the harassment and disarming of the people.

The pigs hope to manipulate the fear and racism of the broad mass of unconscious whites in order to eliminate black revolutionaries, and by black revolutionaries we mean black people in general. Pigs like Alioto wish to maneuver these white people into allowing the fascist army to sweep the ghettos and machine-gun or imprison the people. But anyone who, by their racism and government-manipulated fear, supports genocide makes the grave error of forging his or her own slave chains, and if white people in fascist America don't think they are enslaved they only prove their own foolishness.

The enemy has kept us divided for hundreds of years, and for at least that long the pig has made uncountable attempts at eliminating the rising tide of black revolution. But black people, by their strength and determination, have survived this fascist onslaught. Black people, more revolutionary than ever before, are armed and angry.

And now the SLA is proving that black people ain't alone, that the thing the pigs fear the most is happening, is growing. The people's army of irate niggers of all races, including whites, not talkers but fighters. The enemy recognizes that the people are on the brink of revolution, and the enemy will do anything at any cost to prevent this.

We ask the people, especially whites, to carefully analyze Operation Zebra, the black and white wars of the times, and to understand who in reality sits in the saddle and holds the reins.

Death to the fascist insect that preys upon the life of the people.

the voice of Patricia Hearst (Tania)

Greetings to the people. This is Tania. On April 15th, my comrades and I expropriated $10,660.02 from the Sunset branch of the Hibernia Bank. Casualties could have been avoided had the persons involved cooperated with the people's forces and kept out of the way until after our departure.

I was positioned so that I could hold customers and bank personnel who were on the floor. My gun was loaded, and at no time did any of my comrades intentionally point their guns at me. Careful examination of the photographs which were published clearly shows this is true.

Our action of April 15th forced the corporate state to help finance the revolution. In the case of expropriation, the difference between a criminal act and a revolutionary act is shown by what the money is used for.

As for the money involved in my parents' bad-faith gesture to aid the people, these funds are being used to aid the people and to ensure the survival of the people's forces in their struggle with, and for, the people.

To the clowns who want a personal interview with me – Vincent Hallinan, Steven Weed, and the pig Hearsts – I prefer giving it to the people in the bank. It's absurd to think that I could surface to say what I'm saying now, and be allowed to freely return to my comrades. The enemy still wants me dead.

I am obviously alive and well. As for being brainwashed, the idea is ridiculous to the point of being beyond belief. It's interesting the way early reports characterized me as a beautiful, intelligent liberal, while in more recent reports I am a comely girl who has been brainwashed. The contradictions are obvious.

Consciousness is terrifying to the ruling class, and they will do anything to discredit people who have realized that the only alternative to freedom is death, and that the only way we can free ourselves of this fascist dictatorship is by fighting, not with words but with guns.

As for my ex-fiancé, I'm amazed that he thinks that the first thing that I would want to do, once freed, would be to rush and see him. The fact is, I don't care if I ever see him again.

During the last few months, Steven has shown himself to be a sexist, ageist pig. Not that this was a sudden change from the way he always was. It merely became blatant during the period when I was still a hostage.

Frankly, Steven is the one who sounds brainwashed. I can't believe that those weary words he uttered were from his heart.

They were a mixture of FBI rhetoric and Randy's simplicity.

I have no proof that Mr. Debray's letter is authentic.† The date and location he gives is confusing in terms of when the letter was published in the papers. How could it have been written in Paris and published in your newspapers on the same day, Adolf?

In any case, I hope that the last action has put his mind at ease. If it didn't, further actions will.

To those people who still believe that I am brainwashed or dead, I see no reason to further defend my position. I am a soldier in the people's army. *Patria o muerte, venceremos.*

the voice of Donald DeFreeze (Cinque)

Death to the fascist insect that preys upon the life of the people.

late April, 1974

The SLA moves to another safehouse, a two-bedroom apartment in the Hunters Point neighborhood of San Francisco, located at 1808 Oakdale Avenue.

May 2, 1974

The FBI finds the abandoned SLA safehouse on Golden Gate Avenue (FBI headquarters is located only a mile down the street).

† See page 208 in the Appendix.

DRINK AT YOUR OWN RISK

APRIL 1974

[graffiti left at the abandoned SLA hideout apartment, 1827 Golden Gate Avenue, San Francisco]

WARNING TO THE FBI, CIA, DIA, NSA, NBC AND CBS –
There are a few clues in this bathroom. However, you will have to wait until they are dry.
An additional word of caution: 1/2 (one-half) lb. (pound) of cyanide (potassium cyanide) crystals has been added to this "home brew" – so, pig, drink at your own risk. There are many additional juicy SLA clues throughout this safe house. However, remember that you are not bulletproof either. Happy hunting, Charles.

A New Year's Resolution, January 1, 1974
(Dedicated to manchild Tyrone Guyton)
Is it real?
To load a gun with a magazine of dreams?
NO.
We say fire power to the people
Against the "hire" power of the ruling class.
Who chained
Hired Hands,

Feet,
And genitals.
Our grip on the gun grows stronger,
And theyyyy will no longer
See day.
They'll feel what's real
From a magazine of steel.

Today the locust
    fights the elephant.
Tomorrow the elephant
    will be disembowelled.
        – Ho –

Freedom is the bread of the land.
        – Cin –

Freedom is the will of life.
Patria o Muerte, Venceremos.
        – Tania –

Da da, Oh my
Books, once read, make good bullet-proofing.
Death to the fascist insects that prey on the life of the people.

May 8, 1974

In three vans, the nine members of the SLA drive to Los Angeles late at night and set up a safehouse at 833 West Eighty-Fourth Street in South Central L.A.

May 16, 1974

William Harris, accompanied by his wife Emily, shoplifts a bandolier at Mel's Sporting Goods in Inglewood; Patricia Hearst waits outside in a car. Accosted by security outside the store, they escape after Hearst sprays bullets at the storefront with a machine gun. In their escape they carjack two cars and one van, and kidnap the owner of the van, Tom Matthews, holding him hostage until the next morning (he is released unharmed).

Late at night, the remaining members of the SLA abandon the Eighty-Fourth Street safehouse after they hear news reports on the radio of the Mel's Sporting Goods shoot-out.

WE'RE HERE TO STAY

MAY 17, 1974

[poem attributed to Angela Atwood, found in the SLA safehouse located at 833 West Eighty-Fourth Street in Los Angeles]

Reality
You're hard to find
We've looked a long time.
A new born babe could tell,
They bid you farewell
And stuffed cries of jive in your place.
Face it, Comrade
Now is the time – we're all alive.
Eat it Pig!
In our minds
The bigger the trigger
The better the target.
The cool, calm palm will smear heavy on the hit.
Sucker pay –
MALCOLM, we're here to stay.

May 17, 1974

Posing as hitchhikers early in the morning, Emily Harris and Patricia Hearst carjack a Lincoln Continental from Frank Sutter. Holding Sutter hostage, they buy a used Plymouth Valiant for two hundred and fifty dollars in cash and leave Sutter with his car. Hearst and the Harrises drive around Southern California for the rest of the day.

At four in the morning, Donald DeFreeze, Nancy Ling Perry, Angela Atwood, Camilla Hall, Patricia Mizmoon Soltysik, and William Wolfe invite themselves into a house located at 1466 East Fifty-Fourth Street in South Central L.A. By early afternoon the word in the neighborhood has spread: the Symbionese Liberation Army is in the house, and they are armed with over fifteen weapons, 4,000 rounds of ammunition, and a two-gallon can of gasoline.

Earlier that day, armed officers from the Los Angeles Police Department and the FBI shoot tear-gas canisters into the abandoned Eighty-Fourth Street safehouse; the police find clothes, food, ammunition, and papers left behind by the SLA.

LAPD SWAT teams and FBI assault teams take positions outside of the SLA-occupied house on Fifty-Fourth Street in the afternoon. At 5:44 p.m., after demanding surrender for nine minutes, a tear-gas canister is launched into the house and the SLA start firing on the police. Over nine thousand rounds are exchanged between the police and the SLA, culminating in the house bursting into flames. At 6:50 p.m., Nancy Ling Perry and Camilla Hall attempt to escape from the rear of the house by shooting their way out; Perry dies after being shot in the back and the chest, and Hall is killed instantly when she is shot in the forehead (other SLA members drag her body back into the burning house). The police declare a ceasefire as the house collapses into flames at 6:58 p.m. All of the SLA members in the house die from gunshot wounds or the fire; no civilians, police, or FBI agents are wounded.

Patricia Hearst and the Harrises watch their "comrades" die on live television while sitting in a motel room in Anaheim.

June 2, 1974

Four hundred people attend an SLA memorial at "Ho Chi Minh Park" (Willard Park) in Berkeley.

SIX MURDERED COMRADES

JUNE 8, 1974

[transcript of audio tape]

the voice of William Harris (Teko)

To those who would bear the hopes and future of our people, let the voice of their guns express the words of freedom. Greetings to the people: the Black Liberation Army, the United People's Liberation Army, the Black Guerrilla Family, the Weather Underground, and all freedom fighters of the United Symbionese Federation and the New World Liberation Front.

This is Teko speaking. Yolanda, Tania, and I extend profound feelings of revolutionary love and solidarity to General Field Marshal Cabrilla and all the soldiers of the United People's Liberation Army; to Bitin Commander and all elements of the anti-aircraft forces of the SLA; to Combat Unit Number Four of the Black Liberation Army; to comrade Martin Sostre and all other comrade brothers and sisters in America's concentration camps.

To our beloved comrades-in-arms and prisoners of war, Osceola and Bo, we echo the words you have often left us with: "*A luta continua, venceremos.*"

We have come together in many different cells, squads, and military political units. We have taken many different meaningful names. But we are not hung up on names, for, as comrades-in-arms, we are one in our struggle for freedom. The determination to eliminate our common enemy by force of arms has united us. To our comrade sisters and brothers of the Black Liberation Army and all other fighters, let it be known that the Malcolm X Combat Unit of the Symbionese Liberation Army proudly takes up the banner of the New World Liberation Front.

The Malcolm X Combat Unit of the Symbionese Liberation Army left the San Francisco Bay Area in a successful effort to break a massive pig encirclement. It had become clear through intelligence reports from other SLA elements and from the people in the community that the pigs were preparing to trap us on the San Francisco peninsula. We knew that there was a great risk in setting up a base of operations in San Francisco, which is a natural defile, a trap. The area is very small, surrounded by water, and with limited choices for breaking a major encirclement. However, we accepted this potentially dangerous condition because we saw the importance of making solid contacts in the oppressed communities of this city. We considered ourselves to be an underground unit. However, the majority of our unit's members moved about freely, and, in the five months we were there, we made many good contacts.

We decided to move our base of operations to Southern California, concentrating on the greater Los Angeles area with its vast oppressed communities and more favorable terrain. In April, the War Council dispatched an Intelligence and Reconnaissance Team to Los Angeles. Its mission: to make some additional contacts and survey the area. Based on the favorable results of this mission and the concentration of pig activity in the San Francisco Bay Area, our unit slipped out of San Francisco and into Los Angeles on May Day, 1974.

On Thursday, May 16th, 1974, three members of the Malcolm X Combat Unit of the SLA were sent out to buy a number of items needed by the unit. At Mel's Sporting Goods Store in Inglewood, a pig-agent clerk named Tony Shepard, attempting to show his allegiance to his reactionary white bosses, falsely accused me of shoplifting. It was impossible to allow a verifying search by a store security guard because I was armed, and therefore we were forced to fight our way out of the situation.

The pigs originally said that a forty-nine-cent pair of socks was stolen, and that this was what caused the shoot-out at the store. The people found this very difficult to believe when it was pointed out that we had already purchased over thirty dollars' worth of heavy-duty wool socks and other items. This, apparently, became increasingly confusing to the pigs, who later charged that an ammunition bandolier was the item taken, supposedly to make the accusation more believable.

The policy of the Symbionese Liberation Army has always been to avoid shoplifting because of the heavy risk involved to the whole unit. We cannot afford to have soldiers busted on humbug charges. However, we realize that the combat and support elements run a great risk of being jammed whenever we move about aboveground. The most unfortunate aspect of this situation was that the pigs then learned that SLA elements were in the Los Angeles area. It appears that even with this knowledge, the pigs would not have located our comrades if a collaborator named Mary Carr had not snitched to the enemy.

On Friday, May 17th, 1974, a CIA-directed force of FBI

agents, Los Angeles City, County, and California State pigs, with air support and reserve assistance from the United States Marine Corps and the National Guard, encircled elements of the Malcolm X Combat Unit of the Symbionese Liberation Army. The result of the encirclement was that the people witnessed on live television the burning to death of six of their most beautiful and courageous freedom fighters by cowardly, fascist insects. In most cases, when an urban guerrilla unit is encircled by the enemy, it can expect to take great losses, especially if the enemy has time to mobilize a massive force.

Our six comrades were not on a suicide mission, as the pigs would have us believe. They were attempting to break a battalion-sized encirclement. By looking at the diagrams of where their bodies were found, it is clear that they had split into two teams, moved to opposite sides of the rear of the house, and were preparing to move out of the house by force. The heavy automatic weapons fired from the front of the house was a diversionary tactic to force the pigs to concentrate some of their forces in the front. The two dynamite-loaded pipe bombs were to be used as fragmentation grenades to clear a path through the cringing pigs who had started the blaze by firing incendiary grenades into the house.

Cin, Fahizah, Zoya, Cujo, Gelina, and Gabi died of smoke inhalation and burns before they could get outside. The pigs want us to believe that the fire was started by the SLA, that it was caused by SLA molotov cocktails, or by accident from pig tear-gas grenades. This is pig shit. The SWAT squad, FBI, and LAPD would have had to go into the house themselves to clear it out. They showed their true cowardice by using incendiary grenades to cause the fire that killed our comrades.

For those that don't know, incendiary grenades burn at such an incredible temperature that they melt steel and armor plate in a matter of seconds and are impossible to extinguish.

The pigs want the people to believe that the badass tactics of the SLA guerrillas drove the fascists to use such barbaric force, but we say the SLA is a reaction to fascism. The SLA uses automatic weapons and homemade bombs because the pigs have automatic weapons, artillery, and hydrogen bombs.

The pigs want the people to believe that General Field Marshal Cinque Mtume committed suicide. To this absurdity, the SLA respond by quoting our beloved comrade brother. He often said: "We must not fear death, for to fear death is to put our fear of pig terror before our love of the children and the people's struggle for freedom." The pigs have historically focused on eliminating black leaders. Many have been murdered or imprisoned in America's concentration camps.

For over a year, the pigs couldn't find Cin to murder him, so they attempted to isolate him from the people with pig propaganda. First they worked on the most blatantly racist whites with their traditional, uh, "crazy, black-nigger, escaped-convict-rapist" routine. Next, we learned that Cin was a plum-wine alcoholic. This obviously was the white, racist, liberal answer to the logic that a black revolutionary leader could order and assist in the assassination of a jive-assed, pig-agent school superintendent.

It followed that the white supremacists and bourgeois black elements of the revolutionary left so-called leadership would be pimped with ridiculous tales of links between the SLA and the CIA – that Cin was and had been a paid informer for the

Los Angeles Police Department and the California Attorney General's office. If this were true, we dare these fools and collaborators to explain Cin's reward for his deeds: a life term in California's concentration camps.

White, sickeningly liberal, paranoid conspiracy freaks and spaced-out counterculture dope fiends proved their naivete and amateurish research skills as they rambled on and on and on about the California Department of Corrections. Bizarre stories about Cin having been programmed and electrodes implanted in his brain while at Vacaville began to appear in the so-called underground press.

Cinque Mtume: the name means "Fifth Prophet." Cin was indeed a prophet. The pigs would have the people believe that Cin was just, as they would say, another dumb nigger. They continually attempted to undermine his leadership by propagandizing that Cin was being fronted off by whites, that he wasn't smart enough to be the brains behind the planning and execution of the successful SLA actions.

To this display of racism we say, go on into the black community and ask the people if Cinque Mtume was not a prophet. Ask the people if they think he was being used by whites. The people know that a black man in America does not need conscious whites to push him into leading a revolution. Racists cannot believe that middle- and upper-middle-class whites and a daughter of a super-fascist ruling-class family would ever have reason to follow the lead of a beautiful, black genius, revolutionary warrior and give their lives for the people. Sick-assed racists would have us believe that white women who follow the lead of black revolutionaries are only mindless cunts enslaved by gigantic black penises.

The cringing pigs who faced the firepower of Gelina, Gabi, Fahizah, and Zoya know much better.

Racists believe that it is impossible for white men to denounce white racism and follow the revolutionary leadership of black men, but the SLA proved this theory to be a sick delusion. Cinque Mtume was himself the spirit of Frederick Douglass, Gabriel Prosser, Denmark Vesey, Marcus Garvey, the Scottsboro Boys, Medgar Evers, William E. Burghardt DuBois, Malcolm X, Martin Luther King, Emmett Till, little Bobby Hutton, Fred Hampton, L. B. Barkley, Jonathan and George L. Jackson, Mark Essex, and every other black freedom fighter who came before him.

To racist slander, the SLA and all the people say: death to the fascist insect that preys upon the life of the people.

And now, after our comrade brother fought valiantly against a battalion of pigs – a battle witnessed by millions – these same chicken-shit pigs are trying to have us believe that General Field Marshal of the Symbionese Liberation Army Cinque Mtume killed himself. Cin was so determined to kill pigs that, as long as his heart was beating and that there was any air in his lungs at all, he would fight, even if his only weapon was his own body. We all know that revolutionaries do not kill themselves. Revolutionaries kill the enemy.

Cin was the baddest member of the SLA and therefore our leader. Our five white comrades who died with him were among his students and had learned well. They, too, showed incredible determination and courage. Cujo, Gelina, Fahizah, Zoya, and Gabi did not commit suicide, as the pigs would have us believe.

Pigs tell us it is suicidal for whites to join blacks and other oppressed people in making revolution. To this oinking we say it is suicidal for the ruling class and all its pig agents to believe that they can continue to oppress, exploit, murder, and imprison an undivided revolutionary army of the people. White Americans who follow the example of our beautiful comrades and join the fight for the freedom of all oppressed people will not do so because they wish to die, but because they wish to be free.

The pigs boast that they have broken the back of the Symbionese Liberation Army. But to do this, the pigs would have to break the back of the people. The military/political leader of the SLA and five top cadre have been killed by the fascists. However, the SLA is not dead and will not die as long as there is one living, fighting member of any oppressed class, race, sex, or group left on the face of this earth. The pigs have won a battle, but the war of the flea is not over. As our dear comrade Ho Chi Minh once wrote from an imperialist prison, "Today the locust fights the elephant, but tomorrow the elephant will be disemboweled."

the voice of Emily Harris (Yolanda)

Greetings of profound love to the people, to all comrades-in-arms, to all comrades in the concentration camps in fascist America, and to all the children. This is Yolanda speaking.

When we say revolution, we do not use the word loosely. By revolution we mean the violent fight for freedom, freedom that can be gained in no other way than by fighting. People do not fight because they enjoy it or because they relish the thought of their own death or the deaths of their beloved comrades. They fight to survive, because they understand the violence of fascism, and that violence means genocidal death at the hands of dictators who massed five hundred pigs, armed with military weapons, fragmentary grenades and incendiary grenades, to burn six people to death. Dictators who have imprisoned over twenty-two thousand brothers and sisters in the state of California alone. Dictators who take jobs away from those who are begging to work. Dictators who take food from the mouths of those who are starving. Dictators who take joy from the hearts of those who love the people.

The military/industrial state of the ruling class can only survive through repression. These fascist dogs must destroy truth in the minds of the people to keep them pacified. They must make people afraid so that they will do nothing. They must make people feel isolated from each other and powerless. Fascism tries to do all these things through the brutal violence of the military police force, the lurking big-brother presence of the FBI, CIA, and their computer files, through media propaganda. Fascism tries to tell us we are fools to resist, because we will in the end be destroyed.

If we were only six people, they would be correct, for they can destroy the lives of six, or nine, or even one hundred people. But the truth the pigs try so desperately hard to repress is one the people are coming to understand only too well. People are ridding themselves of the bourgeois desire to lead a long life, and instead wish to fight for a better, more human life. Yes, repression breeds resistance. It is proven to be true as each day goes by, as dark eyes grow darker with hate, and strong muscles grow stronger with rage, and cold steel grows colder in the firm grip of a hand that loves the people.

We must face the inevitable truth that repression will grow more intense as the power-hungry pigs see their grip slipping. Whites in this country have historically had a tendency to back off when repression intensified, feeling they could escape the vicious tentacles. For this reason, black, brown, Asian, and Indian brothers and sisters have not trusted whites, feeling that they would desert the fight as it was just beginning in order to save their own skins. These brothers and sisters were often proven correct. That is why we say anyone who loves freedom must prove this love through action, not words. And only after they have fought can they speak.

So we are freedom fighters. We may be murdered, but whether we live or die, the day is close at hand when the people will join together in an army because they wish to survive on their own terms, and the people will change the course of history through their courage and determination. To all those whose fear is stronger than their hatred of the pig, I must say that the freedom fighters do not bring repression to your door. The fascist pig is responsible for this, and soon even those of you with white skins will lose your privileges.

The pig will no longer knock and be very polite. He will shoot to kill. He will burn and rape. He will imprison and starve. He does this already in the ghettos of this country, and will expand his efforts to stay in his greed-filled position of power. And if people wish to survive, they will have to defend themselves with as much rage as the pig would use against them. Only in this way can the people of this country avoid the mass genocide that occurred to Jews in Germany and leftists in Chile.

All these things have been said before, but I will continue to say them until the reality is so clear we no longer need to repeat the words. That will be the day when our mind accepts what we see with our eyes.

To those who have attempted to express their love for us by calling for our surrender, we say, we must express our feelings of love only by continuing the fight. We renounce our class and race privilege and say that we love no individual more than we love freedom. The fight has cost us, of the SLA, eight comrades: six dead, and two in concentration camps, as well as the death and imprisonment of our comrades-in-arms of the BLA, the BGF, and the Weather Underground.

We clearly understand that the reality of revolution will include death and imprisonment, suffering and violence, as well as victory. The price is high, but we accepted this reality when we picked up the gun for the first time and nodded yes to freedom, to love, to living. Because we must endure the suffering does not mean we have any doubt in the beauty of the victory.

Our comrades died the way they chose to live: fighting courageously. They did not compromise to the hundreds of insects crawling the community who resorted to burning them to death rather than facing in battle the ruthless strength and courage of freedom fighters. Fifty-Fourth Street is not an end, but a beginning. People are gathering on the street. They are feeling the strength of their own bodies. They are clearing the fear and blind ignorance from their eyes. Cinque, Fahizah, Zoya, Cujo, Gelina, and Gabi conquered the fear and will never die in the minds of those who see the monster and know he will be destroyed.

All comrades, dead and alive, in prison and out, underground and on the streets, are calling on all the people to conquer the fear and join the battle, realizing what can happen when five hundred pigs surround a house, and then are surrounded by fifty, or one hundred, or five hundred irate niggers firing from their houses, alleyways, treetops, and walls with a straight and fearless shot to bring down the helicopter, the SWAT squad, the LAPD, the FBI, the neighborhood snitch. Consider the day when the pig won't even enter the communities of the armed people. We got to make the pig fear for his life, because he knows every eye behind every curtain in the ghettos, barrios, and poor communities is sighting down the barrel of a piece, ready to pull the trigger at any moment.

There's been a lot of talk about wasted lives, referring to the six dead bodies of our comrades, and to Tania, Teko, and myself. The ironies of racist, fascist America are once again reflected with sickening reminder. There are no editorials written for the wasted lives of the brothers and sisters daily gunned down in the streets and prisons. The present uproar of white America over the fate of Patty Hearst was barely a murmur, as hundreds of young men, mostly black and brown, went off to die in Vietnam.

We of the SLA hate the historical reality that requires young people to struggle to survive and to die violent deaths. We hate the reality in this country that murdered our six comrade sisters and brothers and daily continues to murder throughout the world. Because we hate this reality, we must fight to destroy it by any means necessary. Yes, history might be different if they had lived, but revolution is not made by saying "if only." We do know that the lives of revolutionaries will never be wasted.

Right now there are men and women, young and old, black,

brown, Asian, Indian, and white who are filled with the fighting spirit of King, of Malcolm, of George, of Cinque, of your mothers, fathers, sisters, and brothers who have died at the hands of the pig. And these are a new breed of the baddest motherfuckers alive. Yes, we hate the pig, and we are at war with the pig, and we will kill the pig as violently as he has killed comrades of ours for centuries. We will do this because we love the people we are lucky enough to know, and we love the people we will never know: the beautiful babies, the angry young men and women, the understanding mothers and fathers who have seen the rising tide for as long as they have been alive.

Our past as middle-class white Americans was meaningless. It was truly wasted potential, filled with desperate pessimism that could feel the emptiness of capitalist America even before we could understand it. Our lives now are not easy or full of joy. We may die. But our lives are real, because we see the truth and the future. Right now the people are igniting the spark for the great prairie fire, and the firefighters will soon be helpless against the freedom fighters because the flames will be far too hot and deadly for their weak will to endure, and their evil spirit will die with them in the ashes.

Once again, my love to all the comrades.

the voice of Patricia Hearst (Tania)

Greetings to the people. This is Tania. I want to talk about the way I knew our six murdered comrades because the fascist pig media has, of course, been painting a typically distorted picture of these beautiful sisters and brothers.

Cujo was the gentlest, most beautiful man I've ever known.

He taught me the truth as he learned it from the beautiful brothers in California's concentration camps. We loved each other so much, and his love for the people was so deep that he was willing to give his life for them. The name Cujo means "unconquerable." It was the perfect name for him. Cujo conquered life as well as death by facing them and fighting. Neither Cujo or I had ever loved an individual the way we loved each other, probably because our relationship wasn't based on bourgeois, fucked-up values, attitudes, and goals. Our relationship's foundation was our commitment to the struggle and our love for the people. It's because of this that I still feel strong and determined to fight.

I was ripped off by the pigs when they murdered Cujo, ripped off the same way that thousands of sisters and brothers in this fascist country have been ripped off of people they love. We mourn together, and the sound of gunfire becomes sweeter.

Gelina was beautiful. Fire and joy. She exploded with the desire to *kill the pigs.* She wrote poetry. Some of it on the walls of Golden Gate, all of it in the L.A. pig files now, that expresses how she felt. She loved the people more than her love for any one person or material comfort, and she never let her mind rest from the strategies that are the blood of revolution. Gelina would have yelled "firepower!" to the people if there wasn't the need to whisper the words of revolution. We laughed and cried and struggled together. She taught me how to fight the enemy within, through her constant struggle with bourgeois conditioning.

Gabi crouched low with her ass to the ground. She practiced until her shotgun was an extension of her right and left arms, an impulse, a tool of survival. She understood the evil in the heart of the pig and took the only road that could demoralize, defeat, and destroy him. She loved to touch people with a strong, not delicate, embrace. Gabi taught me the patience and discipline necessary for survival and victory.

Zoya wanted to give meaning to her name, and on her birthday she did. Zoya, female guerrilla, perfect love and perfect hate reflected in stone-cold eyes. She moved viciously and with caution, understanding the peril of the smallest mistake. She taught me, "Keep your ass down and be bad."

Fahizah was a beautiful sister who didn't talk much but who was the teacher of many by her righteous example. She, more than any other, had come to understand and conquer the putrid disease of bourgeois mentality. She proved often that she was unwilling to compromise with the enemy because of her intense love for freedom. Fahizah taught me the perils of hesitation, to shoot first and make sure the pig is dead before splitting. She was wise, and bad, and I'll always love her.

Cinque loved the people with tenderness and respect. They listened to him when he talked because they knew that his love reflected the truth and the future. Cin knew that to live was to shoot straight. He longed to be with his black sisters and brothers, but at the same time he wanted to prove to black people that white freedom fighters are comrades-in-arms. Cinque was in a race with time, believing that every minute must be another step forward in the fight to save the children. He taught me virtually everything imaginable, but wasn't liberal with us. He'd kick our asses if we didn't hop over a fence fast enough or keep our asses down while practicing. Most importantly, he taught me how to show my love for the people. He helped me see that it's not how long you live that's important, it's how we live, what we decide to do with our lives. On February 4th, Cinque Mtume saved my life.

The Malcolm X Combat Unit of the SLA was a leadership training cell, under the personal command of General Field Marshal Cinque. General Teko was his second-in-command. Everything we did was directed toward our development as leaders and advisors to other units. All of us were prepared to function on our own, if necessary, until we connected with other combat units. The idea that we are leaderless is absurd as long as any SLA elements are alive and operating under the command of our General Field Marshal.

It's hard to explain what it was like watching our comrades die, murdered by pig incendiary grenades. A battalion of pigs facing a fire-team of guerrillas, and the only way they could defeat them was to burn them alive. It made me mad to see the pigs looking at our comrades' weapons, to see them holding Cujo's .45 and his watch which was still ticking. He would have laughed at that. There is no surrender. No one in that house was suicidal, just determined and full of love.

It was beautiful to hear Gabi's father. He understands. Gabi loved her father and I know that much of her strength came from the support he gave her. What a difference between the parents of Gabi and Cujo, and my parents. One day, just before the last tape was made, Cujo and I were talking about the way my parents were fucking me over. He said that his parents were still his parents because they had never betrayed him, but my parents were really Malcolm X and Assata Shakur. I'll never betray my parents.

The pigs probably have the little Olmec monkey that Cujo

wore around his neck. He gave me the little stone face one night.

I know that the pigs are proud of themselves. They've killed another black leader. In typical pig fashion they have said that Cinque committed suicide. What horseshit. Cin committed suicide the same way Malcolm and King and Bobby and Fred and Jonathan and George did.[†] But no matter how many leaders are killed, the pig can't kill their ideals.

I learned a lot from Cin and the comrades that died in that fire, and I'm still learning from them. They live on in the hearts and minds of millions of people in fascist America. The pigs' actions that Friday evening showed just how scared they really are. They would have burned and bombed that entire neighborhood to murder six guerrillas.

The SLA terrifies the pigs because it calls all oppressed people in this country to arms to fight in a united front to overthrow the fascist dictatorship. The pigs think that they can deal with a handful of revolutionaries, but they know they can't defeat the incredible power which the people, once united, represent.

It's for this reason that we get to see, live and in color, the terrorist tactics of the pigs. The pigs saying, "You're next." This kind of display, however, only serves to raise the people's consciousness and makes it easier for our comrade sisters and brothers throughout the country to connect. I died in that fire on 54th Street, but out of the ashes I was reborn. I know what I have to do. Our comrades didn't die in vain. The pig lies about the advisability of surrender have only made me more determined.

[†] Murdered African-American leaders Malcolm X and Martin Luther King, Jr., Black Panthers Bobby Hutton and Fred Hampton, and brothers Jonathan and George Jackson.

I renounced my class privilege when Cin and Cujo gave me the name Tania. While I have no death wish, I have never been afraid of death. For this reason, the brainwash/duress theory of the pig Hearsts has always amused me.

Life is very precious to me, but I have no delusions that going to prison will keep me alive, and I would never choose to live the rest of my life surrounded by pigs like the Hearsts. I want to see our comrades in this country's concentration camps, but on our terms as stated in our Declaration of Revolutionary War, not on the pigs terms.

Patria o muerte, venceremos.

Death to the fascist insect that preys upon the life of the people.

Summer 1974

The Harrises and Patricia Hearst, successfully evading the FBI, go underground. They are transported to rural Pennsylvania to live in sports journalist Jack Scott's rented farmhouse; they later move to another farmhouse in upstate New York and attempt to write a book about their experiences in the SLA.

mid-September, 1974

Patricia Hearst and the Harrises relocate to Sacramento, California.

March 1, 1975

Russell Little and Joseph Remiro attempt to escape from the Alameda county jail; Little stabs Deputy Larry Franks in the throat with a pencil (narrowly missing his jugular vein) and Remiro gouges out the right eye of Sergeant Robert Jensen, but they are subdued by other guards before they can get to the jail's weapons locker.

April 21, 1975

Armed with a shotgun, Emily Harris rushes into the Crocker National Bank in Carmichael, California, with new SLA recruits Kathy Soliah, James

Kilgore, and Michael Bortin; they rob the bank of approximately fifteen thousand dollars. William Harris and Kathy's brother Steve Soliah wait in one getaway car, Wendy Yoshimura waits in another, and Patricia Hearst waits in a third (a few blocks from the bank, near a funeral home). Emily Harris shoots to death forty-two-year-old church worker Myrna Opsahl during the robbery.

June 27, 1975

Russell Little and Joseph Remiro are sentenced to life in prison for the assassination of Marcus Foster. Little's conviction is overturned on appeal in 1981 and he is freed; Remiro is currently serving a life sentence as Inmate #B66003 at the California State Prison in Lancaster.

August 13, 1975

Emily Harris and Steve Soliah blow up a parked police car in Emeryville, California; no one is hurt.

August 20, 1975

Patricia Hearst and Steve Soliah place a bomb near the entrance of the Marin County Sheriff's Office; it detonates later on a timer set by Soliah, injuring no one.

On the same evening in Los Angeles, William Harris, James Kilgore, and Kathy Soliah place a bomb under a police car parked next to a restaurant on Sunset Boulevard; it is rigged to detonate when the police car drives away, but it does not explode.

September 18, 1975

The FBI arrest William and Emily Harris as they begin their lunchtime jog outside of their apartment at 288 Precita Avenue, in the Bernal Heights neighborhood of San Francisco.

Patricia Hearst and Wendy Yoshimura are arrested later in the afternoon while sitting in their kitchen at 625 Morse Street (in the Crocker-Amazon neighborhood of San Francisco). Hours later, Hearst tells the booking officer that her job is "urban guerrilla."

September 24, 1976

Patricia Hearst is sentenced to seven years in prison for her involvement in the Hibernia Bank robbery.

1977

William and Emily Harris begin six-year prison sentences for their roles in the Hearst kidnapping and the crime spree in Los Angeles; after their release, the Harrises divorce. Emily works as a computer consultant for Hollywood entertainment companies; William works as a private investigator in San Francisco, gets married, and raises two sons.

January 29, 1979

President Jimmy Carter commutes Patricia Hearst's sentence; she is released on February 1.

April 1, 1979

Patricia Hearst marries her bodyguard, Bernard Shaw. Her book about the SLA and her kidnapping, *Every Secret Thing,* is released in 1982. She and her husband move to Connecticut, where she raises her two daughters and acts in the films of John Waters.

January 20, 2001

President Bill Clinton pardons Patricia Hearst.

2002

Due to the political atmosphere after the terror attacks of 9/11, and the persistence of Myrna Opsahl's son, William and Emily Harris – with Kathy Soliah and Michael Bortin – are prosecuted for their participation in Opsahl's murder and the Crocker Bank robbery. Accepting plea deals during their trial, the Harrises serve their sentences from 2003 to 2008.

APPENDIX

LETTER FROM DONALD DeFREEZE TO JUDGE WILLIAM L. RITZI APRIL 1970

Dear Sir

I know you may think I am trying to be funny or smart because I sent you a Motion for a recall of a sentence And Commitment and you denied it. I am sending you another one with this letter.

What I want to do is just to talk to you, "Thats all," I want you to hear the truth of everything, you never give me a chance to talk or anything, I am in Jail, but I still want to let you know what really happened and Why.

I am going to talk to you truthfully and like I am talking to God. I will tell you things that no one has ever before know.

To Start a story of a mans life you can't start at the end, but at the start, this start will begain at the age of Sixteen.

At that age, I had Just gotten out of a boys school in New York after doing 2 1/2 years for braking into a Parking Meter and for stealing a car, I remember the Judge said that he was sending me to the Jail for boys because he said it was the best place for me, I was sixteen at the time and didn't have a home, life in the little prison as we called it, was nothing but fear and hate, day in and day out, the hate was madening, the only safe place was your cell that you went to at the end of the day, I only had two frights, if you can call them frights, I never did win, it was funny but the frights were over the fact that I would not be a part of any of the gangs, black or white. I wanted to be friends with everyone, this the other inmates would not allow, they would try to make me fright, but I always got around them somehow, they even tried to make a homosexual out of me, I got around this to, after two1/2 years I found myself hated by many of the boys there.

When I got out of jail, people just could not believe I had ever been to Jail, I worked hard, I didn't drink or any pills nor did I curse, I didn't hang out at night in the Street and I believed in God and really tried to live a good life.

But I was still lonely, I didn't love anyone or did any one love, I had a few girl friends but as soon as there Mother found out I had been to Jail, that was the end.

Then one day, I met my wife Glory, she was nice and lovely, I feel in love with her, I think, I believe I was just glad and happy that anyone would have me the way I was, I was Eighteen and in love and life really became real to me, I asked Glory to Marry me and she said yes, we had just met one month before we were married. My wife had three kids already when I met her.

We were Married and things were lovely all the way up to a few months, then Seven months later I came home sooner than I do most of the time from work and she and a old boy friend had just had relations, I was very very mad and very hurt, but I told the boy he could have her and she him before I killed someone, the boy said he didn't want her at all, she was just another girl to him, we tried it again, as time went on we started to be a family, then one day I found out that none of my kids had the same father and that she had never been married.

I really put faith in her, but somehow little storys kept coming to me, one was that my boss had come to my home looking for me and that my wife had come to the door in the nude, I closed my eyes to it all, I loved her and her kids and I did everything to be a father and husband, I worked hard to give them a home and the things she wanted, but somehow they would never be enough for her.

I thought that if we had kids or a baby we would be closer, but as soon as the baby was born it was the same thing I had began to drink very deeply, but I was trying to put up with her and hope she would change.

But as the years went by they never did and she told me that she had been to see her boy friend and that she wanted a divorce because I was not taking care of her and the kids good enough, I was never so mad in my life as I was then after all I had tried and forgiven. I could have killed her, but I didn't, I through her out of the house and I got drunk I got a saw and hammer and completely destroyed everything I ever brought her and I mean everything, all of it when she came back, there was nothing to come back to!

For months later she came and begged me to take her back she said she had made a mistake and that she really loved me, I was weak again, I took her back and started making another home for her and Our kids But I couldn't face anyone any more, I started drinking more and more and staying at my job late and all the people that lived around us would be asleep, I started playing with guns and firer works and dogs and cars, Just anything to get away from live and I how happy I was I finely got into trouble with the Police for shoting off a rifle in my basement and for a bomb I had made out of about 30 firer works from fourth of July.

I made up my mind to lieve New Jersey and my wife made all kinds of promises to me and begged and begged me to take her.

I moved to California, I put my age up so no one would think about me having so many kids I looked like I was nineteen. I told my wife I would forget all that she had did to me and everything as if it never happened, I treated her like a man should his wife.

But I was wrong again, because more and more I was happy with everything, I started playing with guns, drinking, pills but this time more than I had ever before did. I was arrested again and again for guns or bombs. I don't really understand what I was doing, she wanted nice things and I was working and buying and selling guns and the next thing I knew I had become a thief.

I thought that if I made her a lovely home here in California she would finely wake up and be a wife.

I worked two Jobs and was a trief in between, she has all she wanted, TV's in every room, her home looks like or better than a movie stars, I tried to hind my weakness and unhappiness in work, I worked 22 hours a day and still I had no peace and she wanted more.

You sent me to Chino and I lied to them and didn't tell them all the truth. I think they think I am nuts.

God has told me to go home if I believed in him and changed my life and forgave everyone that had did me wong and I did, my wife also I forgave I kept my promise. But you should have never sent me back to her.

The day after I got home she told me she had had Six relations with some man she meant on the street when I was in

Chino. she said she wanted nothing between us and thats why she had to tell me, I said that I forgave her and I can in some way understand why she did it But I never did, if I love someone I don't want anyone but her no matter what, anyway I thought to myself that God and you had forgiven me, so I must forgive to No Matter how bad it is, and try to make a Marriage.

Sir that didn't last long.

I wanted to get away from her somehow, I said to myself that I would go with them, my wife and kids to New Jersey and help them get things fixed up in there nice home and then come back to California.

My wife started getting on me for more money for this and that and really making me feel like I was crazy, one day I went and took $100.00 from them. I took that money home and gave it to my wife, I through it in her face, I was that mad, she said I was a fool! I could have Stole all of the money which was $1500.00 but I only took $100.00 of it. Sir what she said really did something to me, it opened my eyes to what she was and what she had made me became, that night I got into my car and I drove for two days and nights and came back to Calif. to go to Jail and do whatever time I have to start my life over. I never got a chance to give myself up I was arrested.

Sir Don't send me to prison again, I am not a crook or a thief nor am I crazy, I hope you will believe me, I am foolish. Honest and Truthful, but I was very proud and very weak when it came to my wife. But that's over and gone.

Sir even if you don't ever call me back or want to see me againm Thank you for all you have done and all I can say is God Bless you, Yours truly, Donald DeFreeze

LETTER FROM EMILY HARRIS TO HER PARENTS MR. AND MRS. FREDERICK SCHWARTZ JANUARY 1974

Dear Mom and Dad,

This letter is long overdue and because of that I am sure it will be somewhat difficult to understand. I'm a very different person than you have known in the past, and I have not communicated that difference to you very honestly. I see suffering all around me – people in prison, people working at unfulfilling jobs that earn just enough money to keep them barely alive; people being murdered on the streets just because they are black and standing on a corner. These are realities. These are realities which exist and which you have chosen to ignore in your life. These realities exist because some people insist on being rich regardless of whether they must utilize the blood and sweat of others. I do not see my freedom and happiness as something that comes when I grab as much as I can from someone else. I will never be free until there are no more rich people and no more poor people. This means that I can no longer relate to the aspirations you have for creating a comfortable life for yourselves because they ignore the tortured lives that others lead in an attempt to survive. Just because you appear successful does not mean you are smarter than another person – instead it means you are white, well-educated and willing to ignore reality in order so that you may do better than others at the expense of others.

I've learned a lot from Bill, from other people here in Oakland, and from people in prison and they in turn have learned a lot from me. One person in particular – a beautiful black man – has conveyed to me the torture of being black in this country and of being poor. He had dedicated his life to eliminating the conditions that oppose people's being able to lead satisfying lives and replacing these with conditions that make people truly free – so part of the process is to destroy and part is to build.

Bill and I have quit our jobs and have moved with people who are serious about destroying and building. I feel better than I have ever felt because I see myself as a part of a meaningful process that involves more than just myself as an individual – it involves and will affect the way a lot of people live. If I were alone in aspiring to do this I would have little or no effect. But the fact is that more people are dissatisfied than are satisfied so out of their dissatisfaction grows success for the changes that are necessary and inevitable. Bill and I have changed our relationship so that it no longer confines us, and I am enjoying relationships with other men. I am in love with the black man I referred to earlier and that love is very beautiful and fulfilling. I feel like under these circumstances close communication with you all will only be destructive to us all.

I would like to continue to develop in some of the directions I have described here, and I know that much of this will be alien to you. This leaves us little to say to each other. I am not the daughter that you know from the past and that I have pretended to be in the more recent couple of years. I cannot continue to communicate the things I know you want to hear. I love you because of the independence you gave me in the past to get to the point where I am now, but I realize we are headed in totally opposite directions and we can never hope to turn those around and go backwards to a point in the past where we had something in common. I will keep in touch every once in a while but not regularly. Trust that I am well and filled with many aspirations for the future. I do not do this out of any hard feelings, only practical common sense based on no hopes for any real sharing to take place through our communications. None of the changes in me are sudden, but all are part of a process of realization that began years ago. I am a very strong person who is finally realizing their potential. It is truly a wonderful feeling. I only wish I could share it with you but I would be naive if I thought there was hope for that. One or the other of us would have to negate everything that we lived for. My love for you has not changed, it's just that my love for other people and purposes has far exceeded it. Goodbye to the past, forward with the future.

Emily

P.S. I don't know how you will react to this but I feel you will be upset. Please don't try to project these feelings on me or to interfere in any way. I will write sporadically to let you know that I am well.

BERKELEY BARB EDITORIAL

FEBRUARY 1, 1974

SLA's Fahizah Just Naive by Sgt Pepper

Now that we have a letter from Nancy Ling Perry Fahizah of the Symbionese Liberation Army, we have a "fix" on what's coming down.

Up to this letter, all we had to go on was an incredible series of blunders on the part of the SLA which, in turn, gave us fragments of the movement.

It now turns out to be no movement at all but a naive bunch of Whites acting out their role as Blacks. That's all there is to it, sorry to relate, and what Ms Fahizah adds up to is a frustrated White middle class female who likes to write slogans in her own blood.

Her letter reminds me of early Black Panther communiques. Or the former Stanford revolutionists in Venceramos. (Never repeat never did the Weathermen and Weatherwomen resort to such tactics, ie, assassination; rather, they destroyed property rather than people).

In fact, I don't think she wrote that letter all by herself – it has the earmarks of a speech written for Nixon or LBJ or Reagan. Proof? Her letter is too structured. That is to say, it is perfectly composed as though by a professional, not by a La Passionaria hiding from the cops.

A letter from the real Nancy alone would be more spontaneous, more alive, than, for example "First of all, I think I should tell you of my background and the evolution of my consciousness." She then proceeds to column inches of a Marxist, class-warfare analysis at the time she was in High School in Santa Rosa a pom-pom girl for Goldwater.

If this is what the Senator from Arizona can produce, then why are people worried about what UC Berkeley turns out?

One gets the eerie feeling that Fahizah has been programmed to act this way at this time, either by the FBI or the CIA (see The BARB, "CIA Makes Zombie?" Jan 11, 1974.)

One need not be zapped by drugs or psycho-surgery, however, to get a planned response – look at all the news these days of female couriers used by Palestinians or Moroccans or dope smugglers in Turkey – usually American tourists, "who didn't know" their tape-recorders were time-bombed or their luggage carried five guns and a 150 rounds of ammo, etc.

I personally saw two females get busted five minutes after they held up the Bank of America at Ashby and Adeline – THEIR Svengali got caught in their trailer, money until he was busted.

None of these women were put upon. They were just naive. And this, I feel, is the case of Nancy Ling Perry Fahizah of the Symbionese Liberation Army.

Somebody is using a dedicated fighter for social justice, but she got in too far and blew it. Example: she says she didn't want to burn down the house in Concord but only to "melt" any fingerprints.

Fingerprints don't "melt."

Further: since nobody knew it was there in the first place, if she kept her cool the police would STILL be looking for it. Her action however, called attention to the house.

Her comrades blew their cool too. In shooting at the Concord police that night, they exposed their operation to the cops and public in a rather pathetic light; ie, why wear guns ALL the time?

Her explanation for the armaments gets rather confused as to what is "defensive" and what is "offensive." Here we are, sitting in the middle of a shooting war (according to her) and nobody seems to know about it.

Some of this exposure appears to be calculated. Example: police keep coming up with piles of literature, leaflets, manifestoes, all of which never seem to get distributed to the people.

Who did the printing? Who was to read it? Why didn't it get circulated on the streets?

I was talking with another dedicated street revolutionary a week BEFORE the busts. He expressed wonderment because "there was no mass movement or action in the Black communities" from which this action would flow (like Watts, for example).

He felt that both August Seventh Guerrilla Movement and the Symbionese Liberation Army were "police agents."

Now, we find that Fahizah claims the August Seventh Guerrilla Movement is a "police plot to discredit revolutionaries and confuse people."

And the latest ASGM communique says, "Request from Nancy Ling, A.S.G.M. stands ready to assist, militarily, the remaining units of S.L.A."

What still remains, in all this confusion, is: what was to be gained by offing Marcus Foster – did the CIA "dirty tricks" team expect a crackdown on Bay Area dissidents (who are not dissidenting any more, anyhow) or is the SLA a bunch of sincere people long on revolutionary theory but short on tactics and common sense?

LETTER FROM HUEY NEWTON TO THE HEARSTS
FEBRUARY 14, 1974

THE BLACK PANTHER PARTY
CENTRAL HEADQUARTERS 8501 EAST 14TH STREET
OAKLAND, CALIFORNIA 94621 (415) 638-0195

FOR IMMEDIATE RELEASE
FEBRUARY 14, 1974

Mr. and Mrs. Randolph Hearst
233 West Inez
Hillsborough, California

Dear Sir:

First, let me say, as the leader of the Black Panther Party, that we have no relationship with the Symbionese Liberation Army.

The fact is, however, that Patricia Hearst is already captured by the Symbionese Liberation Army and in danger. In the past, we, the Black Panther Party, had attempted to help the U.S. corporate interests avoid bearing such a yoke, by asking and imploring your help for the people's survival. In this interest, we ourselves gave away over $154,000.00 of free food to poor people, in order to forstall what has presently happened.

Therefore, in the light of the fact that Ms. Hearst's capture and in light of the Symbionese Liberation Army's just demands for free food for poor people, we are willing to help resolve this contradiction.

Because we are familiar with mass distribution of free food, we, the Black Panther Party, are willing to take full responsibility for the distribution of food to the masses of people in exchange for one life, the life of Patricia Hearst.

We will distribute food to the poor, to the oppressed, to the disenfranchised. We will do so as we have always done because we are one with the people, not because we are parties to or victims of extortion.

The rights of the people to the plenty of this land is something we have fought and died for, but we did not die only to become romantic curiosities.

We struggle for the people, for the rights of mankind. We will not involve ourselves in their destruction. We, as always, will struggle for their liberation.

We have known people before, both fascists and fools, who have tried to make of us murderers and kidnappers. They have their motives. But for us, let it be known that we never murdered anyone to make our motives and our beliefs clear.

We believe in the freedom and the rights of man. And we will feed people because we know that people are hungry, not only because we know that some are prisoners.

Huey P. Newton
Black Panther Party

NATIONAL CAUCUS OF LABOR COMMITTEES PRESS RELEASE FEBRUARY 16, 1974

The National Caucus of Labor Committees has now confirmed that the "Symbionese Liberation Army" (SLA) kidnappers of Patricia Hearst, is a front for the Central Intelligence Agency – entirely under CIA and LEAA-affiliated control.

Since it is to the political advantage of the CIA and its masters to have Patricia Hearst killed, following a build-up of national hope for her rescue, her murder is probable unless an immediate exposé of CIA responsibility occurs.

On the basis of information collected from several kinds of sources, including police officers, we have been forewarned of a LEAA/CIA plan to organize ghetto riots and other killings leading up to a crescendo during early March of this year.

From its first appearance of prominence in press coverage during recent weeks, we have been carefully investigating the so-called Symbionese Liberation Army (SLA) as one of the CIA-LEAA instruments for their campaign of terror. This investigation was initiated on grounds of ideological and modus operandi features of this operation.

Further information received during the past 48 hours confirms our initial suspicions. There is no doubt that the SLA is a CIA/LEAA front.

The principle evidence for this falls into two categories. Firstly, reports tracing members of the SLA to programmed behavioral modification units within prisons and similar institutions. The second type of evidence is epitomized by the SLA's use of the "KAWAIDA" symbol and ideology.

The two identified SLA leaders, Donald D. DeFreeze and Thero M. Wheeler, † "escaped" from prison last year. Both were inmates of California's Vacaville State Prison, site of notorious behavior modification programs sponsored by the CIA-run Law Enforcement Assistance Administration. Vacaville inmates are subjected to electroshock of the genitals, drugs which simulate drowning, and other elaborate tortures which make up the "aversive conditioning" routines.

This morning's New York Times reported that the Symbionese Liberation Army was born in special "sessions" and "classes" of an official Vacaville prison program where political training was given.

"Kawaida" is not merely a symbol. Kawaida is a concept developed by Dr. John Rawlings Rees of the Rockefeller-funded Tavistock Institute, the OSS and the CIA.

Kawaida represents a set of indoctrinational precepts which

† Thero Wheeler was an African-American prisoner in Vacaville, and an active member of Venceremos, when he met Donald DeFreeze; they both participated in Colston Westbrook's Black Cultural Association. Much like DeFreeze's effortless flight from Soledad in March 1973, Wheeler easily escaped from Vacaville on August 2; he stayed with DeFreeze, Soltysik, and Perry, and was involved in early discussions about the SLA. When the planned murder of Marcus Foster was broached by DeFreeze and others, Wheeler went into hiding and later took a bus to Houston, Texas.

After Patricia Hearst was kidnapped by "two black assailants" – DeFreeze and William Harris in blackface – the media and police misidentified Thero Wheeler as one of the suspects. Wheeler continued to live in Houston under the alias "Bradley Bruce" until his arrest months later on prison escape charges.

in brainwashing technology would be identified as a "belief structure" to be imposed upon the brainwashed victim.

The Kawaida system is identified with at least two other known CIA operations. Ron Karenga whose "US" operatives murdered Black Panthers on the UCLA campus, and Leroi Jones, who John Rees personally recycled into the CIA's Imamu Baraka in 1968.

U.S. Attorney General Saxbe has apparently smelled a rat in the entire SLA affair. At a news conference on February 14, he suggested that police agencies, knowing the identities and whereabouts of the kidnappers, are derelict in their duty in not attempting to effect Ms. Hearst's rescue and to bring the zombies to justice.

Publisher Hearst, as the aggrieved parent, made the understandable mistake of opposing Saxbe's public statement obviously on the basis of false hopes that one can negotiate successfully with CIA zombies.

The only way that we can reasonably expect that the SLA would be prevented from killing Patricia Hearst is to put pressure and responsibility on the group's masters – the CIA and LEAA. A full press exposure of these and other facts should be made immediately, and full cooperation should be given the Attorney General's office in proceeding to safely extricate the victim from the zombies who are now holding her captive.

We will make any further information which we are able to obtain available promptly to the Attorney General's office.

OPEN LETTER FROM BERNARDINE DOHRN
FEBRUARY 20, 1974

Weather Underground
February 20, 1974

Sisters and Brothers,

A massive morality play of American life is occurring, bringing home the message that this society will necessarily continue to produce revolutionaries, whose essential purpose will be understood by masses of people. It demonstrates that the American Empire is violent, ruthless, and based on oppression.

As the Symbionese Liberation Army action has unfolded, the bare bones of this drama have emerged out of the contradictions and militaristic style: the guerrillas have kidnapped the daughter of a rich and powerful man in order to provide food to the poor. Their action has unleashed an astonishing pactical unity among people's organizations, and a leap in everyone's consciousness about the fundamental reality which will not die or pass into the memoires of a previous decade. That is, the war between the rich and the poor.

There are four points we would offer.

1. American society is maintained by force and violence. The ruling class has held a monopoly on violence and has fed us a steady diet for centuries. Africans were kidnapped and brought

here in chains to labor as slaves; Asians brought to build the railroads and mine the ore, kidnapped during World War II and transported to detention camps; Chicanos brought to harvest the fruit and vegetables; poor whites brought as indentured servants or desperate unemployed – and historically all of us pawns and participants in the theft of Native American land and history.

Two hundred years later, this terror is still both institutionalized and randomly encouraged:

– Last November, three white policemen murdered 14 year old Tyrone Guyton one block from his home in Emeryville. He was black, shot with a .357 magnum pistol.

– Reagan's latest assault, Welfare Regulation No. 6, became effective January 1, 1974. It eliminates people who are technically illegal aliens from the welfare roles of AFDC and medical programs threatening the survival of thousands of Chicano families who have come in search of work. Poor mothers and their children have been singled out to bear the brunt of the attack. At the same time, farm workers are being shot at and arrested for their struggle to organize.

– Ruchell Cinque Magee, a victim of official kidnap since June 1963, is being tried again in San Jose for participating in a legitimate slave rebellion, called "aggravated kidnap" by the authorities. In that rebellion, 17 year old Jonathan Jackson was brutally gunned down by San Quentin guards. His grieving mother had no riches to save her childrens' lives.

– At the present time, the government holds 22,000 people hostage in the California prisons. They are subject to an escalating "get tough" policy of lock-downs, special adjustment centers and indeterminate sentences. When they can't be contained or broken, they are executed as was George Jackson.

– Terror-bombing from the air, the random destruction of the lives of millions, has been the Asian – and now African – experience of Pax Americana.

For two generations, the Hearst newspapers themselves have wielded their power and profits by exploiting the most lurid aspects of war, irrational violence, and racist and sexist ideas. They have a lot of reckoning to account for.

2. We support the right of people to food. Shadowing the more blatant terror is the silent violence of malnutrition, forced sterilizations, and schools which teach children to be illiterate. This secret form of murder is increasing and it is systematic.

Hunger and the need for food are urgent. The fact that there are enough people in need in California to require $400 million to feed them for one month reveals the dimensions of the crisis. And this is the cornucopia of the United States.

Look at Vietnam, formerly the rice bowl of Southeast Asia. Now the Saigon-controlled areas of South Vietnam are in the midst of a rice famine. This is the consequence of a US-sponsored decade of savage interference in the Vietnamese right to self-determination and independence. It remains true that in Vietnam, US priorities can be seen most clearly. Last year Nixon gave $1.3 billion in military aid alone to Thieu.

3. There have always been attempts to disassociate extremists from moderates, to rewrite the fierce struggles of yesterday into "reasonable" unthreatening squabbles, and – above all – to incite

racist fears about what might happen when *"they"* get out of control. It is the people who make revolution, and they must determine how and when revolutionary violence is necessary. This is fundamental: the oppressed have a common enemy. Don't do the enemy's work. The media distort and denounce in an attempt to divide the revolution. Movement spokespeople who react to political crises by asserting their own moderation and legitimacy are providing ammunition which will be used in the ruling class plans to split and weaken us.

Beware of the familiar phrases used against every kind of revolutionary action: "it's premature", "it turns people off" (some people), "it brings down repression". The same words are used to attack sit-ins, draft-card burnings, urban rebellions, the struggle of women, G.I. revolts, or occupations of institutions. Whether or not any of this is literally true, the important thing about revolutionary action is its political effect, its direction, what it teaches and changes and strengthens.

Today Nat Turner and John Brown are considered revolutionary heroes. In their own time, each was attacked as a murderous lunatic by the more "respectable" abolitionists. Revolution is officially revered only in retrospect.

It is a new experience for us to be described as a moderate alternative in the Hearst press. This has never happened before. New Left "moderation" is invented now as another racist weapon against Black revolution.

Despite the efforts by the media to sow confusion, many organizations and leaders have kept the primary issues of official violence and oppression in the forefront, affirmed the serious intentions of the SLA, and called for food for people and the safety of both Patricia Hearst and members of the SLA. This is a new and beautiful development.

4. Revolutions are uneven. They develop from concrete conditions. Like people, like nations, they are each unique and yet share common qualities. They will not behave according to expectations; they are forged in grinding suffering and resistance.

For the ruling class, it's an easy thing to anonomously destroy thousands of lives. The use of violence carries different burdens for conscious revolutionaries who love the people, than for their enemies who fear and hate people.

We do not comprehend the execution of Marcus Foster, and respond very soberly to the death of a Black person who was not a recognized enemy of his people. But it is wrong to allow such questions to become a grant of immunity to enemies and executioners of the oppressed. The system always holds that its massive violence is legal and moral and that revolutionary violence by the people is illegal and outrageous. It is the opposite that is true.

The hypocrisy of ruling class morality and justice is shown in their treatment of the SLA prisoners. Joseph Remiro and Russel Little have not been tried, but they are being held in isolation in the Adjustment Center of San Quentin. And still the three policemen from the same area who murdered a 14 year old Black manchild have not even been indicted, despite the collective outcry of the Black community.

Committed political workers will be criticizing and discussing the Hearst kidnapping for a long time, but we must acknowledge that this audacious intervention has carried forward the basic public questions and starkly dramatized what many have come to understand through their own experience: It will be necessary to organize and to destroy this racist and cruel system.

for the Weather Underground,

Bernardine Dohrn

LETTER FROM COLSTON WESTBROOK TO DONALD DeFREEZE

MARCH 4, 1974

Dear Brother Cinque,

You sure did come down hard on ma man in that last tape. Uuummhh did you ever do it. In fact, I really felt sorry for the cat. Yea, the communication gap is just great. No rich white man is going to know how to talk to a nigga, especially a pure nigga. But, maybe a bousie nigga and a pure nigga can rap a bit.

Cin, I had a feeling that sooner or later you would be free, and whenever I heard that you were on the lam – I was not surprised. But when asked if I wanted to help – well, I am sure that you got my reply. What other reply could I give to a brother who needs help – yet does not trust me? I could have snitched, but I am not a snitcher. Neither are you. And believe it or not, I am not a pig. Can you dig it brother?

Dig it Cin, I think that I can understand your Symbionese thing and know that you will not harm Patty unless the man makes a bum move. They don't know you as I know you, but as you said – they know you. Obviously, however, the POlice, the feds, and the news media are greenhorns when it comes to using and understanding Black Communications. Yea, what do they know about repartee in the black culture? What do they know about prisoner psychological rhetoric? What do they know about black speech techniques such as "puttin' a dude down?" But, they have tried other things such as trying to goat you into makin' some stupid telephone call. Well, they got the public's sympathy, but once again they underestimated your intelligence.

How's Patty? I know that this situation must be a little bit rough for her, but I hope that she takes out a little time to think about her studies at CAL. Did you tell her about your UNISIGHT thing. Yea, do you remember the night when you asked me if you could have some time on my program so that you could do your UNISIGHT thing? I gave it to you. The brothers didn't want to give you the time, but I did.

Went up to Vacaville on Thursday to brief the Super about this news thing I am doing. I really like him because he will make time to talk to anyone if it is important enough. Tried to get some of the mainline gossip; no one ain't saying nuthin. But, I did hear the cats crackin' jokes such as: the guerrillas got a gorilla with them. I don't think TW looks that bad. He studders a bit and has reading problems, but I surely don't think he looks like a gorilla. Does he still like to smoke the same kind of cigars that you like? Say, dig this: I got a mug shot of him with Russ and me in it? Wow, dynamite, huh. Sorry, I didn't mean to say that word; don't want to trigger anything.

Regarding your "good faith" demands of providing food for poor people, I thought that it was a brilliant move on behalf of your leader; he anticipated the anticipated. Personally, I think that something must be done about the welfare situation not only in the State of California but in the entire United States. Not bad thinking for a bousie, huuhhh? So, maybe the pressure being exerted on the Hearst zaibatsu will make the public aware of poor people's needs. Undoubtedly you heard some of the psychological games being played about people not accepting the food. But let me tell you sumpin' Bro, many of the niggas are hongry. And the most severe PIN situations are the senior citizens and recently-released prisoners.

OK, yes, I do not agree with what you are doing, but I do understand it. I am somewhat surprised, however, that your demands did not direct any attention to the fact that black prisoners seem to serve more time than any other prisoners. And don't you know that because of this SLA thing that the BCA has been suspended? And don't you know that a lot of brothers got denied because of your SLA trip? Yea, I know, they most likely would have gotten denied anyways. But, why add fuel to the fire?

Look Cin, I am not making a plea; I just want to talk to you man-to-man, brother-to-brother, nigga-to-nigga. Can I help, and if so – how? It is not necessary to talk to me directly – unless you want to. I suggest that messages be relayed to me through any one of the following people: Nge, Yohana Mwasi, Uhuru, Mpata Kufanya, Mshala, Mpagazi, Mchawi, Mwezo, or – The Chui. As you know, they are still down, and all of them know Ramee or Kale-na-Kale. If that route is difficult to use, I still maintain limited contact with Dhati, C.X., and Flim-Flam at "Q." And yea, Kinye Kilaminajaro is there too. And aside from these people, maybe some of the brothers "down home" such as Oba Fahali, Ishmael, Mwalimu Kikanza or Nyoka will help out. But, maybe you will want to communicate via a brother who has risen. That's mellow too.

Well, I am getting hungary now. My main squeeze is going to make some ribs with beans and rice, but I sure do wich that I had some "kimchee" to go with it.

Later,

Big Daddy aka Yajiuma

P.S. . . . Say Cin, I dig your Field Marshall rank; too bad you couldn't be a Messiah.

BERKELEY BARB ARTICLE

MARCH 22, 1974

What To Do When The FBI Comes

1. Look before you open the door.

2. Don't let FBI or police in without a warrant.

3. DON'T TALK. No law requires that you talk with FBI or police. Lying to any federal official is a federal crime.

4. Note down names, badge numbers, license numbers, physical descriptions, etc. Tape record when possible.

5. Ask your friends, relatives, and employers to not cooperate and to let you know if they've been contacted.

6. If you need legal help and don't know a friendly lawyer, call the National Lawyer's Guild: 285-5066.

7. Stay cool. Stay calm. Stay SILENT.

LETTER FROM VICTORIA HEARST TO HER OLDER SISTER PATRICIA HEARST

APRIL 5, 1974

Dear Patty,

We miss you, very much. We want you back, unharmed.

I hope your captors allow you to read this. I think it only fair that they allow you to hear both sides.

I want to assure you that Dad has done everything in his power to help you. At no time did he ever wash his hands of you. He loves you. We all do.

The S.L.A. says that they are acting in response to the needs of "the people." Well, I'm part of the people, too, and I have a very great need. I need my sister. Patricia Hearst is not a symbol of the "fascist middle class." She is a human being, and as such she has a right to life. If the S.L.A. denies her that right, they commit a crime not only against this family, but against Humanity.

Patty, we're all hoping that you'll come home very soon. I think that this thing has been carried on long enough. The S.L.A. has made their point. The time has come to break the silence and negotiate. Until that happens, I hope you can hang on, and remember that we love you and want you back.

All my love, Vicki

LETTER FROM RÉGIS DEBRAY TO PATRICIA HEARST APRIL 12, 1974

Paris, 12 April, 1974

To Patricia Hearst

I just received a visit from your friend Steve. It is at his request and only responding to considerations of human solidarity that I take the liberty to intervene, on a personal level, in a situation in which the spirit, methods, and intentions are obviously foreign to me.

Steve let me listen to your last message in which you say you have exchanged your name with that of Tania. The name of Tania – or Tamara Bunke – is an integral part of our revolutionary patrimony. It has a deep and grave resonance for all the national liberation movements of Latin America. And for me also – because I had the honor of working and fighting with her until the last moments of her life, in Bolivia. It is because Tania was a comrade and friend that I want to speak to you. The enemies of socialism and revolution have done everything, as always, to spoil the memory of this German Communist militant who freely chose to die at Che's side in the interests of the people of Bolivia. You will understand that we must be cautious to protect the moral integrity and the international purity of her commitment.

As a French citizen the internal affairs of the United States do not concern me. And the only purpose of this message is to contribute to the clearing up of any ambiguity on your real situation, and to relieve the anguish of your friends who fear for your safety and your life. It is not up to me to judge the reasons and the opportunity of your personal choice. I ask you only to assure me that you have consciously and freely chosen to take the name and follow the example of Tania. If such is indeed the case, we can do nothing but respect your decision – no matter how questionable it may seem.

But on the other side, there is something that Tania's comrade could not accept – that anyone should dishonestly and cynically, without your agreement, disfigure the memory of a militant who could not have sacrificed herself for the cause of an oppressed people, victims of undevelopment and an atrocious military dictatorship, deprived of all legal means of expression and resistance, as is the case of the Bolivian people and such other people in Latin America, without having lived several years amongst the workers, without having studied with application the theory of scientific socialism and the reality of the actual world. It was only a long and difficult apprenticeship which permitted Tania to create her own revolutionary morale. I hope you will understand the human sense of my intervention.

If there is a reason of security for yourself or for those in your company that impedes you to appear personally in public, I am sure that, following the example of all the serious and responsible revolutionary movements which operate in secret because they are compelled to, you will find a way to deliver to an anonymous intermediary, without needless publicity, irrefutable proof of your free and conscious choice. This intermediary can be any common friend of Steve and you.

Good Luck, Patricia

Régis Debray

BLACK PANTHER PARTY PRESS RELEASE

APRIL 18, 1974

THE BLACK PANTHER INTERCOMMUNAL NEWS SERVICE
8501 East 14th Street Oakland, California 94621 (415) 638-0195

PRESS RELEASE

FOR IMMEDIATE RELEASE
WED. APRIL 18, 1974

CALIFORNIA REFUSED TO EXTRADITE SLA'S DEFREEZE

(Oakland, Calif.) – Repeated requests for the extradition of Donald D. Defreeze, reputed leader of the Symbionese Liberation Army (SLA), while he was in California police custody by New Jersey police officials for a 1965 kidnapping and assault with a deadly weapon charge, were denied by California police officials, according to very reliable sources.

Attempts to determine from Los Angeles police files the status of the extradition request has revealed that Defreeze's file, along with those of Larry and George Stiner, recent "escapees" from San Quentin prison, are under lock and key in the safe of the Watch Commander of the L.A. Police Department Criminal Conspiracy Section.

Our sources point out that the above information tends to confirm earlier suspicions that Defreeze is, in fact, an agent-provocateur, under the direct and personal supervision of California's Attorney General Evelle J. Younger – a California "plumber" of this state's Watergate conspirators centered in the L.A. Police Department Criminal Conspiracy Section.

Our sources insist that Defreeze's assignment is to create conditions in Oakland and the general San Francisco Bay Area whereby the Black Panther Party and its leadership, headquartered in Oakland, can be made scapegoats for criminal and terrorist activity for which it has no responsibility.

Our sources further point out that the March 28 alleged "escape" from a maximum security prison of the Stiner brothers, is part of the Younger plan of attack against the Black Panther Party, using individuals with criminal records holding long-standing grudges against the Party. The Stiners were serving time for the 1969 murder in Los Angeles of Black Panther Party members Bunchy Carter and John Huggins.

POEM FOR MIZMOON, FROM MIZSUN
UNDATED

Mizmoon, a Sister who loves you is speaking.

You and I lived Berkeley lives so much alike
that I often ask myself, "what kept me here?"
"what pulled you where you are?"

I'm who you've been and where you came from,
living in the neighborhood,
taking care of kids,
working for a living,
5 political meetings a week, some studying, some
demonstrations,
and some good times with the women and men I love.

Once you loaned me a book, you probably don't remember,
and since then your gifts to me have been many.

I have a memory of you that sticks in my mind:
A year ago, in a meeting, someone asked you,
"why the name Mizmoon?"
and you said, "My lover was speaking poetry to me,
and called me Mizmoon. It seemed perfect for my name."

I really liked the way you said that,

the way you chose your new self the way we each will:
a bold transformation, defying definition,
letting yourself be named by a woman,
a woman who loves you.

Mizmoon, listen!
Don't believe those who say
you're separate from the people,
because you came right out of our lives.

Mizmoon, listen!
Don't deny your past, for its our present.
There was good in everything we ever were.
There had to be, for you created yourself
out of our common past.
Bring us all along with you,
and remember everything you've ever learned.

You are my future.
Show me what I can do,
but remember what I'm doing now.

And Mizmoon, listen!
Even though it seems like there are only a few of us
who are armed,
remember that there are hardly any non-combatants left now.
Most of the people are fighting back in some small way every day.

And Mizmoon, thank you!
You've begun to claim what is ours.
The Robber Barons have stolen and stolen and stolen from us,

wealth and food and work and sex and land and life.
You've taken back a little food for empty bellies
and a little cash for the survival of a part of our Army.
For this beginning, thanks, Mizmoon.

Mizmoon! A Sister who loves you is speaking!
What I want to give you is the unconditional love
of one revolutionary for another.
Its unconditional love that Amerika can never give its children
and its unconditional love that we need
and must give to each other.

No matter what happens, I love you.
If you survive and fight for years until victory, I love you.
If you are captured, wounded, imprisoned, tortured, I love you.
If you are duped and tricked, infiltrated and led to defeat,
  I love you.
If you die a violent death under the guns of the enemy,
  I love you.
If you make more bad mistakes, fail and do us all harm
I'll know that you've tried and lost like many others,
not yet wise enough, not yet loving enough.

I'll struggle with you, I'll criticize you,
but I'll never deny you,
for you are of me and I am of you:

Women.
In struggle.

THE ORGANIC ARMY OF REVOLUTION COMMUNIQUE

UNDATED

COMMUNIQUE TO ALL MEDIA
From: The Organic Army of Revolution.

I am Information Minister and General Field Hand, Pulque, of the Organic Army of Revolution, (OAR.) We think it is time we stuck ours in. Our symbol is the seven-headed artichoke plant.

The OAR has determined that it is time to join the fight for liberation. Up to this time we have lain fallow, waiting. You cannot stop us. Our tendrils are everywhere. We will grasp the enemy in our claws. We will grind him to a fascist paste in our mandibles. Your police can't stop us. Your Army and Navy can't stop us. Your Air Force can't stop us. Not even your stop signs can stop us. We drive right through them like they weren't even there.

The OAR is the first completely organic, grass-roots army in history. Our roots are everywhere and yet we can never be weeded out, because no soldier of the OAR knows the identity of any other soldier. He dosen't even know the identity of his superior officers.

This is made possible by modern electronic media. All orders will be given in the form of communiques to the press. When this is not possible, they will be given on call-in TV shows, radio talk shows, and, if we are lucky, Dialing For Dollars. If the fascist media cuts off this line of communication we will use the telephone and write letters.

CAUTION: TO ALL COMBAT UNITS. When sending communiques through the mails, *don't put your return address on the envelope!* The fascist pigs are clever and can glean valuable information from the most trivial clues.

INSTRUCTIONS TO ALL COMBAT UNITS: When issuing communiques to the media, intentional miss-spellings and gramatical errors should be included to disguise the true educational background of the sender. Exception: If the sender has little or no education or IQ, his communiques should be models of correct spelling, impeccable grammer and erudite language and include quotes from great literature and profound insights, with footnotes and an appendix if appropriate.

Our Revolutionary scientists are, even now, in underground laboritories, working on a new communication system involving an ingenious tape recorder that plays a message and then destroys itself.

SUBJECT: So-called CINQUE of the so-called SLA. Our underground organic grape vine informs us that "Cinque" is a sociopath, a natural actor who cannot feel love or guilt, but who builds up guilt in others and uses it to manipulate them. He thinks he lives in Westworld. His so-called soldiers, are merely his dupes, or "marks" who do not know that he is moonlighting as the Zebra. (Despite his protestations to the contrary.)

The Zebra slayings are, in the opinion of the OAR, deplorable. While we are in basic agreement with their methods, we must dissasociate ourselves from their goals. Though we cannot deny the efficacy of senseless slayings, the Zebra slayings have certain overtones which can only be called, de facto, racist.

To correct this inequality, we are instituting a new series of equal-opportunity senseless slayings. They will be called the new (or Gnu) slayings. The Gnu slayings will differ from the Zebra slayings in that white people will only be killed on even days of the month. Black people will be shot on odd days. Other minorities, as usual, will have to fend for themselves.

SUBJECT: DEATH WARRANTS. Two John Doe death warrants are hereby issued on the following traitors to the Cause: (Their names are witheld to protect loyal associates.)

Below are two composite pictures of the traitors:

If you see anyone resembling these pictures, they are to be SHOT ON SIGHT. WARNING: They may be wearing disguises, do not be fooled by beards, skin color, etc.

It is not necessary, however, to execute anyone under 4 feet tall or over 6' 7" Or people under 11 years of age or over 65.

WE ARE NOT KIDDING

As a demonstration of our strength, and to show that *we mean business,* we have kidnapped a rare specimen of *montia perfoliata* from the Botanical Gardens. If our demands are not met and our message printed in *full* by the media, the prisoner will, if it has not already gone over to our side, be *SHOT*.

DEATH TO THE FASCIST TYPWRITER RIBBON THAT RUNS OUT DURING THE COMMUNIQUES OF THE PEOPLE!

FULQUE

POEM IN REMEMBRANCE OF THE SLA

UNDATED

WE CRY AND WE FIGHT!

We have a right to cry for our dead,
for every life is unnamably precious
and the death of even one woman or one man
who loved the human race
is an intolerable loss.

Only the frozen robot rulers of Amerikkka
have no tears for human suffering.
Only the fascists watch gleefully when people die.

For us, the life of each comrade is everything,
and is always remembered.

Someone somewhere thinks today of every fallen comrade:
of each of the thousands killed in 1927 at Shanghai,
of the vanguard at Moncada,
of the Vietnamese sapper blown up inside Bien Hoa.

Someone somewhere cries today for every fallen comrade:
for Che and Tania,

for Malcolm, George and Jonathan,
Fred Hampton, Sam Melville,
Diana, Ted and Terry,
Sandra Pratt, Zayd Shakur, Twymon Myers.

The memory of our immortal sisters and brothers
helps us to find our tears and rage.
Today our weeping and our anger are for
Fahiza, Cinque, Mizmoon,
Camilla, Willie, and Gelina, gone into History with the others.

Our grief is real, and it makes us stronger and more human.
Our rage is real, and it makes us righteous and powerful.
We cry, but keep on moving, building, loving!
We cry in the night and go to see Ruchell in the morning!
We cry one day and defy the grand jury the next!
In the dark of the night we put our arms around our friends to comfort them
and in the dark of the night we spraypaint with them!
We turn our grief for the dead into love for the living
and write a letter to Assata! (346 W. 20th St., N.Y.)
We cry for our comrades, and we step into their places!

WE CRY AND WE FIGHT!

LETTER FROM BETTY HARRIS TO HER SON WILLIAM HARRIS
NOVEMBER 8, 1974

To the Berkeley Barb:
I am the mother of Bill Harris, who along with his wife Emily and Patty Hearst have been the objects of an F.B.I. manhunt for nine months. I have a short statement I would appreciate your printing in hopes that it may in some way reach my son. The statement is as follows:

Teko, I, along with all your family, panicked after the May 17th massacre. Then I was able to hear the June 7th tape in its entirety and could begin to understand your total commitment to the fight against oppression of all kinds. I have purposely said very little to any members of the media so please understand that any quotes attributed to me are probably figments of someone's imagination.

You are always in my thoughts and I am proud of you. Mostly I hope you will remember the last thing I said to you as we drove away from you in Oakland in January – I love you.

Betty — Carmel, Ind.

If this can be printed I will be so appreciative. Placing it in our local paper seems so useless.

LETTER FROM PATRICIA SOLTYSIK'S BROTHER FREDERICK TO WILLIAM HARRIS

DECEMBER 13, 1974

Six months have passed since May 17. I ask now as I asked then, why did six people die on 54th Street?

My sister died on her birthday. My sister did not choose to die on that particular day. The confrontation was forced. The LAPD, not the SLA, chose the time and place. That was a serious error.

The fatalism which the popular press ascribed to those six comrades represents a dangerous fabrication, a romantic fiction which allows you, Bill Harris, to minimize your responsibility and offers you the luxury of an assuaged conscience. The LAPD chose the time and place because of an "error." Bill Harris, whose judgment failed, whose comrades consequently died?

And what has happened to the ideals so strongly espoused? Has machismo taken priority and have those ideals been sacrificed? I would hope not. But the self-pity and terse eulogies I heard after May 17 suggest otherwise. I would want to believe that on the anniversary of her birth Zoya need not have received your gift.

Frederick M. Soltysik — Goleta, Ca.

BLACK PANTHER PARTY EDITORIAL
SEPTEMBER 29, 1975

Soldier Tanya?

So, Tanya, born Patricia Hearst, much sought after "soldier" of the alleged revolutionary army that claims responsibility for the brutal murder of black Oakland Superintendent of Schools Marcus Foster – the same army that suffered the flaming deaths of five "close comrades-in-arms," sails into custody with clenched fist and broad smile, signing "Urban guerrilla, self-employed."

Strange, how after the murderous assault on the "safe house" in Los Angeles in June of last year, the publicly stated threat by Tanya and her mentors William and Emily Harris that they would die fighting rather than be taken by the armed might of "the fascist insects," and the caches of weapons found in their "safe house," all went so smoothly – almost as if it had been planned.

Have you ever seen a black person arrested in this country? Have you ever seen the treatment reserved for a black American even suspected of being any kind of revolutionary, militant, or guerrilla? George Jackson, Malcolm X, Martin Luther King, Jr., Fred Hampton and scores more are all dead. Yet, these children of the white establishment come floating in on the wings of general good cheer and are sprayed with bouquets of yellow roses.

Are we expected to take seriously U.S. District Court Judge Oliver J. Carter's revocation of bail at the preliminary hearing last week?? By the time you read this "Patty" will probably be ensconced in the Hearst family mansion atop one of San Francisco's several hills.

This silver spooned "urban guerrilla" was so frightened when FBI agents and cops pounded on her back door that she literally wet her pants as they entered, pistols apologetically drawn. No matter. These servants of the "fascist insects" were kind enough to permit her to change into dry pants before escorting her out of the house and into the waiting, chauffered car that would take her to her post-underground television debut.

Be on guard all you who misguidedly aided this quartet in its 19 month flight. Your honest concerns for justice and naive commitment to revolution have unwittingly made you prime targets.

STATEMENT FROM EMILY AND WILLIAM HARRIS

AUGUST 31, 1978

Today we take full responsibility for our participation in the first political kidnapping in this country – the kidnapping of Patricia Hearst. We are entering guilty pleas to what the judicial system calls "simple kidnapping" but nothing about our actions today or those of four and half years ago has been simple. So it comes as no surprise to us that our feelings today are complex – pride in affirming what our actions accomplished and what we learned from them; a very definite pain that 6 of our close friends died, Russ and Joe are in prison and the two of us will be separated from each other by years in prison; a relief that the uncertainty of the past years is over; and a confidence in our combined strength to continue fighting for the principles we believe in – the right of all people to control their own lives and to be free no matter what the costs.

We participated in an act which removed Patricia Hearst from her home, her way of life, the people she knew and the privilege which had insulated her from the oppression that so many people suffer. Out of all the lies, distortions, exaggerations that have emmanated from the Hearst family in an attempt to fool the public – one fact alone has been true. Patricia Hearst was kidnapped. She was *not* brainwashed, beaten, tortured or raped. She was *not* locked alone in a closet for days and weeks on end.

She was *not* coerced into rejecting her family and remaining with the people who made up the SLA.

She was kidnapped by a group of 8 SLA members. Our politics had various origins – the prison movement, the anti-war movement, the women's movement – but all developed at a time when the Nixon White House was attempting to crush all forms of legal dissent thru infiltration, surveillance, murder, break-ins, frame-up criminal charges. The 8 of us along with others in this country responded by translating our beliefs into illegal armed actions as a means to attack power and wealth. We were fully aware of the risks – death, imprisonment, failure – but we all felt totally committed to any and all vehicles of change that could propel us closer to uprooting oppression and realizing a free society.

Our actions in 1974 forced the Hearst family to funnel 2 million dollars worth of food into the poor communities of California. The sanctuary of invisibility that the ruling class has so long enjoyed in this country was shattered. The source and extent of the Hearst's wealth was exposed thru the channels of their own media empire and put in brutal contrast to the poverty of millions of people.

At one time Patricia Hearst felt the same pride and self-respect as we did because all three of us saw the events of February 1974 as a coming of age – a leap in our understanding and growth. But since her arrest, she has never allowed herself the pride of confronting the truth and taking responsibility for actions she made of her own free will. Likewise her family and other members of the ruling class will never take responsibility for the oppression that the very existence of wealth and privilege makes inevitable.

A plea does not represent bowing down to the state. It does not mean that we have been given any favors. We have *not* offered them anything. We have only made the pragmatic choice of accepting what they offer because, very simply, its the vehicle by which we have gained control over the amount of time we will do in prison – the means by which we can be back on the streets the soonest.

Being tried on the State's terms according to their distorted sense of justice and fairness, we would have been found guilty of participating in the Hearst kidnapping. But the State's objective was far greater than demonstrating our involvement in that act – they intended to bury us alive under 13 charges carrying a penalty of life without possibility of parole – a sentence that's been called the living death. Their objective was not grounded in the acts we were in fact responsible for but rather a desire to see our ideas – our revolutionary committment – locked away for life.

Today we take responsibility for 4 acts which is translated into 4 1/2 more years in prison – 3 more years beyond our present term. Within 4 1/2 years we'll be back on the streets where we definately want to be. In this sense we have succeeded in forcing the state to back down.

Our plea today will allow us to speak out on our own terms about the kidnapping of Patricia Hearst – we will be able to share the truth as we know it about the SLA and Patricia Hearst's involvement. We will be able to openly analyze the accomplishments, the failures, the history, the context from our personal perspective. Many of these facts would have come out in a trial but not on our terms. The arena of the courtroom wrenches events out of context, makes some admissable and some not and covers everything with the fog of unreality that passes for justice.

But why was the state forced to make these concessions to us? First, they had very real fears about the credibility of their key witness – Patricia Hearst. They could not separate the truth from the lies and they knew we could. They were dealing with the unknown and we had the facts. Second and probably more important, the State has been alligned with the Hearst family all along – the State with its judicial system is in fact an arm of those who possess wealth and power. We believe the State was forced to back off its objectives in order to protect Patricia Hearst and the Hearst family. In defending ourselves against a sentence of life without possibility of parole, we would have torn apart the web of lies Patricia Hearst has spun ever since her arrest. We would have exposed how the truth of the conditions she lived under after her kidnapping, her relationship to those who had kidnapped her and her feelings about her family all fit together with her decision to remain with the SLA. The humiliating and devastating exposure of the truth would have proved to be a serious setback for the Hearst campaign to get Patricia Hearst released from prison immediately. Also, we would have pursued in the courtroom what the Hearst kidnapping only began – exposure of the Hearst family's history of greed, manipulation of public opinion, open advocasy of racism and championing of imperialist aggression throughout the world. We believe the so-called impartial judicial system was forced to negotiate with us because ruling class interests were at stake. Finally, the State "bargained" with us to save the thousands of dollars that our trial would have cost.

We approached this trial with only the power of our revolutionary committment and we enter our plea today on that basis. This same committment by the SLA in 1974 forced concessions from the Hearst family in the form of food and access to the media. In 1977 the two of us forced concessions from the courts by using their own judicial system to fight for and win appointment of our own lawyers. Our plea today represents even further concessions on the part of the State. While they are forced to back off the brutal thrust of their objective, they are still in a position to extract a price – 4 1/2 more years in prison for us. Like anyone, we experience doubts, pain, sadness and lonliness in confronting this but our feelings exist within a pervading sense of strength, knowing that "time" can't destroy the sense of freedom that's within us.

Valuable years of our lives will be defined by the cold reality of separation from each other, our families, our friends; isolation in maximum security (again a penalty for our ideas, not the acts we are convicted of); degradation of being treated as less than human; violence that spreads like a disease from the racist, sexist hatred of reactionary guards and prisoners. For us this will leave permanent scars but its merely a short term loss while our gains are long term – the historic accomplishments of the Hearst kidnapping can never be erased and we will return to the streets as two strong individuals still committed to change. Ironically the State has only the short term gain of locking up our bodies while they extract their price. The long term loss will always be theirs because they cannot destroy us or the revolutionary potential of the American people.

SELECT BIBLIOGRAPHY

Anspacher, Carolyn, ed. *The Trial of Patty Hearst.* San Francisco: The Great Fidelity Press, 1976.

Berkeley *Barb,* 1973–76.

Burrough, Bryan. *Days of Rage: America's Radical Underground, the FBI, and the Forgotten Age of Revolutionary Violence.* New York: Penguin Press, 2015.

Hearst, Patricia Campbell, with Alvin Moscow. *Every Secret Thing.* Garden City, NY: Doubleday & Company, 1982.

McLellan, Vin, and Paul Avery. *The Voices of Guns.* New York: G. P. Putnam's Sons, 1977.

Payne, Les, and Tim Findley, with Carolyn Craven. *The Life and Death of the SLA.* New York: Ballantine Books, 1976.

Pearsall, Robert Brainard, ed. *The Symbionese Liberation Army: Documents and Communications.* Amsterdam: Editions Rodopi N.V., 1974.

San Francisco *Chronicle,* 1973–76.

San Francisco *Examiner,* 1973–76.

Schreiber, Brad. *Revolution's End: The Patty Hearst Kidnapping, Mind Control, and the Secret History of Donald DeFreeze and the SLA.* New York: Skyhorse Publishing, 2016.

Soltysik, Fred. *In Search of a Sister.* New York: Bantam Books, 1976.

Toobin, Jeffrey. *American Heiress: The Wild Saga of the Kidnapping, Crimes and Trial of Patty Hearst.* New York: Doubleday, 2016.

Weed, Steven, with Scott Swanton. *My Search for Patty Hearst.* New York: Crown Publishers, 1976.

West, Don, and Jerry Belcher. *Patty/Tania.* New York: Pyramid Books, 1975.